No More Excuses!

No More Excuses!

An almost
too-practical
guide to
reading
through
your Bible

Pam Gillaspie

Armor Books
Lawrenceville, GA

No More Excuses by Pam Gillaspie

Published by: Armor Books
P.O. Box 1050
Lawrenceville, GA 30046
www.armorbooks.com

First Printing: September 2002

Cover design: Dave Gillaspie of IMPACT Productions

International Standard Book Number: 1-55829-226-8

01 02 03 04 05 8 7 6 5 4 3 2 1
Printed in the United States of America

With love to
Nannie and Papa

The grass withers, the flower fades,
But the Word of our God
stands forever.
–Isaiah 40:8

Contents

Acknowledgments

I am humbled when I think of how many people God has used to help teach, shape, mold, and support me in this project and throughout the years leading up to it.

For reading, previewing, and giving opinions, thanks to: Debbie Boerman, Ann Milligan, Jan Priddy, Awilda Ibanez, Nicole Ibanez, Kellie Indlecoffer, Beth Hart, Marcia Furrow, Don Tremper, Charlie Howes, Dr. Alan Johnson, Dr. Brian Moulton, Rev. Greg Spencer, my in-laws, Dr. and Mrs. Gerald Gillaspie, and my parents, Dave and Sue Olson.

Thank you to the ladies who study Precept with me on Wednesdays at Immanuel. You all have inspired and encouraged me week in and week out! I wish anyone having a hard time understanding what it is to be part of the body of Christ could spend a morning with us. I love you guys!

Thank you to Kay and Jack Arthur and their wonderful team at Precept Ministries International. I refer specifically to Precept several times in this work and often allude to concepts that I have learned through this ministry. If you want to know your Bible inside out and backwards, and better yet, learn how to take that knowledge and apply it, find a Precept class near you today. Seriously, call 1/800-763-8280 toll free or find them online at www.precept.org. You'll work hard, but you'll never regret your choice of investing in God's Word.

Thank you to my church family at Immanuel; you have helped me to discover and use my spiritual gifts, and have helped to establish me in the Lord over the years. A special thank you to Karen Corlew for pushing me to use my gifts as God intended instead of running from them, and to Debbie Boerman for investing time in me and helping me to develop those gifts.

As it turns out, putting a book and contract together is more complicated than I thought! Thank you to Mike Janiczek and his staff at Armor Books for believing in this project and giving me excellent direction at every turn. Also, a special thank you to Jamey Campbell, Alan Cox, David Treadwell, and Wendell Bird for helping to guide me through the contract maze.

Cress VanderMeersch and Janet Taylor, what would I do without you? Thank you so much for your encouragement and your eagle eyes on the manuscript. More than that, thank you for your incredible friendship over the years. Ben Ondo and Kari Perkins, thank you for your awesome designs and layout.

Mom and Dad, you have modeled to me what God is like. How can I ever thank you? Mom, in you I have seen the way Jesus must have acted towards people. I have never met anyone as giving and patient as you. Dad, in you I have had as close to a perfect picture of God the Father as any human father could be. You have always been a rock and shelter.

Finally, to my husband Dave, for having the guts to step up and be the spiritual leader in our house . . . a hard job for any man anywhere, but even harder when your wife knows Greek. I am honored to follow your wholehearted and godly leadership. Thank you for being willing to give it. Thanks, too, for the awesome book cover!

Brad and Kate, you truly are gifts from God. I pray that you will grow to love our Lord and Savior and His Word with whole hearts and follow Him fully.

Above all, thank You my Lord and Savior for everything . . . You are the Alpha and the Omega, the beginning and the end, from everlasting to everlasting, You are God!

Foreword

For just over twenty years I have enjoyed a relationship with God through my Lord and Savior Jesus Christ. Coming to Christ in the throes of a university education was a rude awakening of a delightful sort. Yet what lingers in my mind since that dormitory decision for Christ is the dominance of God's Word—its power as it convinced my humanist self that life is vanity without God, and its power to reform this growing believer who still clashes with the old self.

That's where *No More Excuses* comes in, because this book is about THE Book . . . how to discover consistency in active Bible reading, and through it hear God's communiqué. General Joshua commanded the congregation of Israel, "You shall meditate on it day and night. . ." With a relational flair, Pam Gillaspie offers numerous helpful solutions to answer the question, "How can I achieve what Joshua has commanded?"

Toward the close of his life, Moses, a prolific author of biblical literature, wrote, "Take to your heart all the words with which I am warning you today, which you shall command your sons to observe carefully, even all the words of this law. For it is not an idle word for you; indeed, it is your life" (Deuteronomy 32:46-47).

Use this book to get into God's Book. Our prayer is that God will use Pam's suggestions to lure those who know God back to vital Bible reading. Indeed, the Bible is classic ancient literature, stylistic and intricate. Yet the Bible reveals His-story, and one cannot examine the story of God's relationship with mankind without encountering life change and spiritual increase.

Therefore enjoy!

Brian K. Moulton, Ph. D.
Christian Heritage College
El Cajon, California

Introduction

I found myself stammering, searching for the proper response to a simple question: "So you've read the whole Bible, right?" The question came from a new believer, a high school junior, who I was discipling through the student ministry at our church where I had been a leader for several years. I could tell by her eyes that the question was not meant as a trap, but in it I was convicted and cornered. For while I had read all of the New Testament several times in college, and had read most of the Old Testament as class assignments along the way, I could not answer Alicea with a simple, "Yes." In that qualified answer, I felt the weight of duplicity. Here I was verbally and mentally assenting to a faith, giving it credence with my tongue, but obviously not enough importance to engage it with my time. And I knew better. That morning at McDonald's, God used a girl named Alicea to show me that while I knew a reasonable amount about the Bible, I had yet to truly experience its life-changing power in my life.

I left Alicea that morning knowing that I needed to make it through the Bible. There could be *no more excuses*! It's not that I hadn't tried before. Like so many others, I had read Genesis and Exodus countless times, stalling in the first few chapters of Leviticus. Over the course of the next year, however, I read through each and every page of my worn New American Standard Bible, by God's grace breaking through five barriers that had kept me from my goal. Since that point, I have made it a goal to read through the Bible every year, alternating among a few translations from year to year. Do I always make it in exactly a year? No. Sometimes I make it quicker, other times more slowly because I am studying specific areas of the Bible in-depth. But my life goal is to follow wholeheartedly the God of the Bible, and I simply can't figure any other way to do that than to be constantly in the God-breathed Word He has given to us.

This book is not intended to be a major theological treatise. It is simply a word of exhortation, a word of encouragement. Yes, I do have some background in biblical studies, but if you're looking for my work number, you're not going to be calling the offices of a university somewhere. I'm home with my kids wiping noses and bottoms (almost done with the bottoms). It's taken me well over two years to crank out a manuscript that Kay Arthur could have written in a weekend. My house has a perpetual problem with Dalmatian hair, we have at least one foot injury a day from stepping on a toy that is in the middle of the family room floor, and trust me, I'm not sitting around eating bon-bons and reading my Bible every day while a housekeeper does the toilets! Believe me, if I can make it through the Bible, then so can you!

Part One: Foundational Issues

Who Wants Me in the Bible? Who Wants Me Out?

My heart grieves for the Church of Jesus Christ. My heart grieves at the lack of knowledge of the truth, at the lack of hunger for the truth, at the lack of endurance in pursuing the truth of God. And I ask, "Why, why do God's people ignore His Word? Why do they not pursue Him and learn about Him and serve Him as He calls?"

Why did I ignore His Word for so many years, when I knew better? Why can it be so hard to read the Bible? Why was I so lax when I knew in my head the truth? Honestly, these can be hard questions to answer. But let's take it back one step further to questions that I believe we can answer simply, logically, and definitively:

Does God want His people to read the Bible?

Yes

Would He make it too hard for you to understand, if He truly wants you to read it?

No

Would God give you the idea that you are not bright enough to read His Word?

No

Would God give you the idea that you are too busy to read His Word?

No

Now, thinking logically here, if God does want His people to read His Word and has made it accessible to the common man and woman, in whose best interest would it be to plant thoughts in your head that would keep you away from the truth *about* God that is directly *from* God? It would be in the interest of Satan, the enemy of our souls.

Destructive thoughts like these come from our enemy. He is the father of lies and has lied from the beginning. Do you know how to combat lies? You combat them with the truth; the truth that is found in the

Word of God. Is it any wonder that our enemy wants to keep us out of the Bible?

It is interesting to me that in the Garden of Eden the lie was "You'll be as smart as God." Now, the lie is "You are so dumb, you'll never be able to understand the Bible." So when we pare it all down, we are left with the question: To whom will we listen? Will we listen to the voice of God who wants only the best for us, or will we listen to the voice of the one who wants to destroy us? Like it or not, that is the choice.

. . . in the Garden of Eden the lie was "You'll be as smart as God." Now, the lie is "You are so dumb, you'll never be able to understand the Bible."

To whom will you listen?

Do I Really Have to Bother?

Sure, you say, maybe it is the enemy who wants me out of the Bible, but I've believed in Jesus. Does it really matter that much? Should I really bother? Do I *really* need to read the Bible? These are valid questions, and answering them honestly is crucial. Let's face it, nowhere in the Bible does it say, "Read the Bible and thou shalt be saved."

What gets us right with God is faith in His Son Jesus Christ, not adhering to a set of rules, such as going to church, praying three times a day, or reading through your Bible once every year, every five, or even every ten. Most people who would term themselves "Christian" know this and therein lies the question: If faith alone saves, does reading the Bible then become optional?

How important is it to obedience? Any thinking Westerner has to ask, "Why should I invest my time here?" "Hey, I listen to Christian radio, have Christian friends, I even read Christian books and magazines, I have good influences in my life, and there are only so many hours in the day. . . does reading the Bible really matter?"

To answer the question of "Why bother?" we need to consider the core issues of belief and salvation, of what it means to have a relationship with God. How does a person get right with God in the first place? How does a human being who does wrong things from the moment he enters the world get right with a holy God whose standard is perfection? How can we as sinful people be set free from sin and death?

If we are Evangelicals, for example, who believe that it is faith in Jesus that saves us, we need to ask, "Where does that concept come from?" The Bible, you say, and you'd be right. Maybe you were taught John 3:16 as a child, "For God so loved the world, that He gave His only begotten Son, that whoever believes in Him shall not perish, but have eternal life."

Maybe you were implored as a child to say a prayer and to ask Jesus into your heart, told that the prayer saved you and that no matter what, you were now going to heaven when you died. Throughout your adult years, you've looked back to that day as the evidence of your salvation. You've driven in a stake to which you can look back and have written in your Bible the date back then when you believed in Jesus. Is this saving faith? Good question, and one which the Bible answers, but to find the answer you have to get into the Word.

In short, if we are pinning our hopes of eternity on a saving "faith" in a God who has revealed Himself clearly to man, we'd better be pretty careful in making sure we understand what it is that He has revealed instead of simply taking the word of another.

Have you ever played the child's game "Telephone"? You probably remember it. A person on one end of the room whispers a phrase to another person, who in turn whispers to another and another. By the time the phrase makes it across the room, it rarely resembles what was initially said. When we look at issues of eternity, we are dealing with extremely high stakes. We need to know what the Word of God says for itself, not just what another person tells us, because there are many very sincere and compelling people out in the world who are heading to hell and taking others with them.

We need to know what the Word of God says for itself, not just what another person tells us.

Each day when I pick up my son at school, I chat with a very sincere woman who is a Jehovah's Witness. She goes door to door and spends hours a week at her "church." Yes, she is dedicated, but she is also deceived.

Because she is so thoroughly deceived, she spends her life unwittingly trying to deceive others. Are her good intentions going to save her? Absolutely not. Her heart has bought a lie about Jesus. Sure, she thinks He's great, but she can't accept that He is God. This mistake has an eternal cost.

While such groups as Jehovah's Witnesses and Mormons clearly miss the salvation taught in the Bible, we still need to look at the Christian Church in America today and ask, "What does true salvation look like?"

If you're wondering whether the concept of true salvation is really an issue, you need look no further than the visible church. Like it or not, the church today is in crisis. Within the walls of the professing church we see daily the ravages of divorce, of drugs, of greed and bitterness, of dishonesty and lust. As the internet stretches its tentacles into more and more households, we see pornography beckoning to our base lusts not from corner magazine stands in public, but from a simple "Click Here" button on our very private computers. It calls to our spouses and our children. Evil has always been pervasive, but today it chases us like never before, and it is evident within the visible church.

This is a problem, and not just a theoretical one. It is a problem because it does not align with what the Word of God says about people who are part of God's Kingdom. Unpalatable as it may seem, God's Word makes it clear that people who have God's salvation show evidences in their lives of the hope that is within them; they bear fruit in keeping with salvation. This does not sit well in our "I'll-do-just-as-I-please" western culture.

Now, I promised that this was not going to be a theological treatise, but we need to see the issue at hand here: Much of the Protestant Church today has bought into a Christianity that is not Christianity at all. They have bought the old easy believism heresy. They have taken the word of another that all you need to go to heaven is to believe in Jesus—which is true. But they have failed to search the Scriptures for themselves to find out what *true belief* looks like. I fear for the visible church today, for those who assent to the facts of the Christ-event with their minds, but whose hearts are far from God, who profess with their mouths a faith in the Gospel of Jesus Christ, but who have never truly possessed salvation.

I fear for the visible church today, for those who assent to the facts of the Christ-event with their minds, but whose hearts are far from God, who profess with their mouths a faith in the Gospel of Jesus Christ, but who have never truly possessed salvation.

I speak here from a Protestant background, having seen from within how easy believism devastates. But for my Catholic friends, your branch of the Church totters on the other side, thinking that people can work their way to God; believing that Jesus is important, but that the good works people do help Him out. Of course a life devoid of works shows a condition of the heart; yet, our work is a mere response to the work that was wrought in Christ Jesus. We are bankrupt. Our works are bankrupt. The currency is bad, like taking a child's play money to purchase a car. Our works will never open the gates of heaven. The only work that will get us in is the work of Christ on the cross.

If we say that we follow Him, we must know what His Word says. We can't live by something we don't know.

This is why we need to bother with the Bible! Because in the knowledge of Jesus Christ, we find all that pertains to life and godliness, and it is in the Word of God that we come to know the person of Jesus Christ. If we say that we follow Him, we must know what His Word says. *We can't live by something we don't know.*

Why are We Biblically Illiterate?

Much of the visible church today does not know the Word of God. Yes, the visible church contains those who drink in the Word, who meditate on God's precepts, and who study to show themselves approved unto God as Paul speaks of in his letter to Timothy. But do the whole-hearted make up the majority of people who show up on Sundays? I doubt it. While we would never mouth the words, when we ignore the Word of God we shout with our very lives, "I DON'T NEED GOD. I can do it better myself. My time is best spent somewhere else." I know this is unpleasant to hear, but is it not truth, my friend? With our computers and PDAs, our e-mail and wireless, we have forgotten the only connection that we really need, the connection with our Creator through His revealed Word.

The logical questions, then, become, "Why are we as a group biblically illiterate, and what can be done about it?"

Consider for a moment the parable of the Sower of the Seed:

The Parable of the Sower from Luke 8

When a large crowd was coming together, and those from the various cities were journeying to Him, He spoke by way of a parable:

"The sower went out to sow his seed; and as he sowed, some fell beside the road, and it was trampled under foot and the birds of the air ate it up. Other seed fell on rocky soil, and as soon as it grew up, it withered away, because it had no moisture. Other seed fell among the thorns; and the thorns grew up with it and choked it out. Other seed fell into the good soil, and grew up, and produced a crop a hundred times as great." As He said these things, He would call out, "He who has ears to hear, let him hear."

His disciples began questioning Him as to what this parable meant. And He said, "To you it has been granted to know the mysteries of the kingdom of God, but to the rest it is in parables, so that SEEING THEY MAY NOT SEE, AND HEARING THEY MAY NOT UNDERSTAND.

"Now the parable is this: the seed is the word of God. Those beside the road are those who have heard; then the devil comes and takes away the word from their heart, so that they will not believe and be saved. Those on the rocky soil are those who, when they hear, receive the word with joy; and these have no firm root; they believe for a while, and in time of temptation fall away. The seed which fell among the thorns, these are the ones who have heard, and as they go on their way they are choked with worries and riches and pleasures of this life, and bring no fruit to maturity. But the seed in the good soil, these are the ones who have heard the word in an honest and good heart, and hold it fast, and bear fruit with perseverance.

"Now no one after lighting a lamp covers it over with a container, or puts it under a bed; but he puts it on a lampstand, so that those who come in may see the light. For nothing is hidden that will not become evident, nor anything secret that will not be known and come to light. So take care how you listen; for whoever has, to him more shall be given; and whoever does not have, even what he thinks he has shall be taken away from him."

–Luke 8:4–18

Before we move forward, let me give a word of encouragement. The very fact that you are reading a book to learn how to read the Bible for yourself says a lot about you. It says that you desire to read the Word, that you're seeking to follow God. You may not have been successful in the past, but the reading of this book shows a heart at least bent in the right direction. I say this here, because the words that follow may seem harsh to those souls of sensitive conscience. However, I fear *not* saying them because we live in the age of the seared conscience, the age of tolerance, and political correctness where nothing is wrong and everyone is "okay."

In light of this parable, though, I would propose that everyone is not okay. Jesus Himself interprets the parable for us, telling us what kind of person each type of soil represents. Let's look for a moment, by way of application, at some of the general categories of and reasons for biblical illiteracy. Considering the four types of soil, we can make reasonable application to the following four types of biblically illiterate people we see in the church today:

"Just Taking Up Space" The Seed Along the Path – Okay, so it doesn't sound too politically correct, but some churchgoers simply take up space. They attend in order to see and be seen. Maybe they're looking for the networking potential or like the sound of "church member" on a resumé. They come to please spouses or parents. Some have “always” come and just keep coming. Nothing gets through to them; they’re annoyed when the pastor preaches one minute over his allotted time. Noon kick-off is infinitely more important than worship of the true and living God. They take up space and nothing more. They are not saved and make no claim to be. They are simply “there.” Unfortunately, people in this category often become hardened and inoculated against the Gospel message. They have heard it and by not accepting it, continue to reject both the Gospel and the Author of salvation. They’re biblically illiterate because they don’t give a rip.

“The Easy Believers” The Seed on the Rocky Soil – There’s another group that usually shows on Sundays; however, many just visit once or twice every few years. They are the easy believers. They’ve bought a non-biblical salvation, a fire insurance that sounded great at the time of sale. It’s all about “asking Jesus into your heart,” and going about business as usual. It’s assenting to a set of facts and living just like you’ve always lived. This group only has part of the story, because they only really want part of the story. They want what is sometimes termed “cheap grace.”

Tragically, in response to the social gospel of the early 20th century, which presented a non-biblical, works-based salvation, Christianity in the late 20th century swung in an over-reaction towards an easy believism. The Church today still suffers the results of this swing as seen in the biblically illiterate who believe that they were saved by a recitation of words, almost an "incantation" of sorts, as opposed to a relationship with Jesus. They often make a profession and then just as quickly as they were "saved" vanish from the scene. The easy believers are illiterate because they think that salvation is fire insurance and theirs is bought and paid for. They hear only that which tickles their ears and otherwise refuse to be burdened with the Word.

"The Encumbered" The Seed on the Thorny Soil – Quite possibly the saddest lot of all are the encumbered. They hear the Word, they *know* it's true, but the "stuff" of life gets in the way. They are too busy to study the Word. They can't find the time in the midst of their jobs and investments and worries and mortgage payments and boats and cars. Could it be, too, that some also cannot find the time in the midst of their ministries and "doings" for God? A big God who desires a relationship and obedience simply does not fit into the crowded lives of those who are encumbered. The encumbered are biblically illiterate because they will not, and eventually cannot, shed the encumbrances to make time to mature.

"The Immature" The Seed on the Good Soil which has not yet grown – Many in our churches are biblically illiterate because they are babes or small children in Christ. My friend, because you have chosen to read this book, my guess is that you fall somewhere into this category, somewhere along the continuum between newborn Christian and the maturity to which the author of Hebrews calls us to press on towards. I'm on the continuum, too. I certainly have not yet arrived, but I am pressing on, and my heart is that you will too.

When my daughter was three she couldn't read a lick, but I knew she would soon because she desired to learn. She so wished she could pick up a book like her older brother and go to it. In fact, she often made up her own stories that matched the pictures in her books in order to move in the direction of reading. I was not downtrodden that Kate couldn't read. I read to her and encouraged the growth, knowing that with the proper nurture, she would inevitably grow mentally and be able to read, just as she continually grows physically. Children mature. Babies grow up. That's just the way life is. And that's just the way spiritual life is as well. We are born as babes. Although enlightened by the Holy Spirit to understand the truth of the Gospel, spiritual babes often arrive biblically illiterate unless they happen to have had some church background prior to regeneration.

Immaturity is not a problem if it is a stage through which one passes.

Is there anything wrong with being a baby? No way! Babies are cute and lovable. They need to be cared for and nurtured. Nothing wrong with being a baby either physically or spiritually. Immaturity is not a problem if it is a stage through which one passes. Some in our churches today are simply baby Christians, and are biblically illiterate because they have not yet learned what they will as they mature in Christ and read His Word. They're starting to learn, they just haven't quite arrived yet. They will, however, grow and bring forth a crop, because all who are truly saved bear fruit. Not all bear the same amount, *but all bear fruit.*

Asking the Tough Question

Your hang-ups in trying to read the Bible may very well be due to spiritual immaturity, you may be an infant in Christ who simply has never been taught some of the basics of getting into the Word of God. You may have other issues linked to this immaturity; such as simple problems of discipline, like a person who finds it hard to get up in the morning to go running, or another who can't put down the doughnut or bag of chips.

It's possible, however, if you have been in the church for a length of time without ever interacting with the Bible, and you're reading this book not because you desire the Word, but you just think that reading is the right thing to do, that your problems with the Bible may go deeper to more core issues of what it means to be a Christian. Don't shut me down here; if you find yourself disagreeing, make a note of it in the margin and resolve to examine the concept as you read through the Bible for yourself.

We know from hearing the words of Jesus that many who listened to Him simply did not "get it." He described them as having ears, but not hearing, as having eyes but not seeing. Throughout the Bible we encounter people who try outwardly to look like they are following God, but whose hearts are far from Him. They encounter the Word of God, but for whatever reason, it does not take root and bear fruit.

I remember back in my college days having to read certain scholarly books on the Bible written by men whose names were followed by a veritable alphabet of credentials. They knew more *about* the Bible than you could even imagine, but they did not know Jesus. The Bible to them proved academically challenging, but spiritually they could not open its pages; they did not have eyes to see or ears to hear, because they didn't know Jesus. He was to them an interesting human being, but they could not grasp Him as being divine. The Gospels were not God-breathed, in their opinion, but merely the result of many different editors, or redactors as they call them, who added and changed and essentially made up most of the Gospel story.

Reading the works of such academics tears my heart, because it is obvious that after spending an entire lifetime pursuing knowledge of the Bible, they themselves are on their way to a Christless eternity. Understand here, that this is not an attack on biblical scholarship. Biblical scholarship done by men and women who know Jesus as their Lord and Savior are a *treasure* to the church; biblical scholarship apart from a relationship with the Author, however, is pointless.

So, you're asking, how do these people relate to me? Here are some questions for you to consider: Is it possible to interact with things of God without knowing God? Is it possible to be a member of the visible church without being part of the real church? Quite honestly, we could debate our theories all day, but the only place where the true answers lie is in the Word of God.

Is it possible to interact with things of God without knowing God?

Jesus, Himself, says that there are those who will cry out to Him, "Lord, Lord," and will not enter the kingdom of heaven. That being the case, can we ever *know* that we are saved? Absolutely. Can we be deceived by our enemy into thinking we are saved, when we are not? You bet. If this were not so, we would not have the call in the Bible to examine ourselves to see if we are, in fact, in Christ Jesus. The Apostle John would not have had to write his first epistle in which he explains how we can *know* that we have eternal life.

The Gospel of John clearly tells us that if we belong to Christ, He will not lose us, that no one can snatch us out of His hand. The question, then, I believe, is not if we can lose what we have, but have we ever had it in the first place. *And knowing God in a saving manner is the basis for any meaningful interaction with Scripture.*

How to Know if You Know Him

So, can you know if you really know Him? Can you know for sure if you are the seed that has a true root? If you study for yourself, I believe you will come to the conclusion that the Bible not only calls us to examine our own lives to see if we are truly saved, but that it gives us some very clear guidelines for such a spiritual examination. The whole point of the book of I John is that its readers might know that they have eternal life, as John says in the conclusion to this letter:

> *"These things I have written to you who believe in the name of the Son of God, so that you may know that you have eternal life."*
> *–I John 5:13*

Take a few minutes to read through the book of I John (located in Appendix A) in the back of this book and ask yourself the following five questions:

1. Do I have fellowship with the Father?
2. Am I abiding in Him?
3. Do I practice sin habitually?
4. Do I have God's love; do I love the brethren?
5. Am I overcoming?

Sound simplistic? Sound judgmental? Maybe, but those are God's questions, not mine. As much as we'd like to pin our salvation on a simple altar call and prayer, the Bible maintains throughout that true belief results in changed lives.

In a nutshell, then, if you have never experienced growth in your spiritual life, if God is only a weekend acquaintance, if you live in bondage under sin (anger, bitterness, addictions, sexual issues, you name it), if you just can't stand the people at church, if you're being crushed under the weight of this world, and you just can't seem to buy a victory, maybe—just maybe, the reason your Bible is a closed book to you is that you have never been truly saved. If you think you may fall into this

---

As much as we'd like to pin our salvation on a simple altar call and prayer, the Bible maintains throughout that true belief results in changed lives.

---

category, it's time to put down this book, pick up your Bible, and read through the Gospel of John. Follow that up with the book of Romans and the Epistle (letter) of I John and I'll meet you back here when you're done! For the rest of us, let's move forward; we too have some Bible reading to get to.

Ingesting the Word

While there's no way of avoiding the fact that plowing through the Bible will take anywhere from 60 to 100 hours of reading time depending on your speed, there are difficult ways to go about it and easier ways. I've tried difficult ways and failed, time and time again, but eventually have found some strategies that have worked very well for me.

Before we jump into some of the "how-tos" of reading through the Bible, I need to make a couple of things very clear. As I relate some of the tricks and techniques I've used in reading through the Bible, they may have a less than "spiritual" ring to them. Don't let this hang you up. My goal here is simply to help you start to put the raw material into your brain. As you get into the Word, God will engage you.

Here's the point: The power is in the Word of God. The power is not in you and does not come from you sitting in the lotus position and thinking sweet thoughts while you read; the power is in the Word. And sure, maybe we do better when we can input it in a contemplative setting, free from the worries of the world, but let's face it, if we wait for the perfect opportunity to meet with God, we may never meet with Him. But if we begin to ingest the Word, even in less than perfect situations, God will use it to change us and draw us to more quality time with Himself. I think back to the testimony of Kay Arthur, who tells of her extreme thirst for the Word after she came to Christ at the age of 29.* She tells of driving her car and reading the Bible . . . talk about less than perfect reading conditions!

If we wait for the perfect opportunity to meet with God, we may never meet with Him.

I often think back to my high school and college days just prior to final exams. I was always one who was studying all night long, drinking Mountain Dew and Jolt, pushing to get every last bit of information into my system. Even though I had been studying throughout the semester, I just didn't want to leave *anything* on the table. It never failed that on a pre-test day I would run into a marginal student who would tell me, "Oh, I'm just going to go to bed early so I'm rested for the test." Now, I've also known great students who sleep instead of studying late, but that's because the info was already in there; my data was never thoroughly stored that early. I would always think to myself: "A rested mind void of information is never going to produce a test answer. I may be a little

* Kay Arthur, a noted Bible teacher, author, and speaker, is co-founder of Precept Ministries International.

groggy going into the test, I may not have put everything in under the most perfect of circumstances, but if it is in there, it can be called upon." Do you see where I'm going here? We need to get the Word of God into our hearts and minds. If our Bibles stay closed for the lack of perfect circumstance, it is not going to happen.

Now, I'm not saying that we use the Word to change ourselves. That would be way too much pressure, particularly because it is an impossible undertaking. As a recovering perfectionist, I can tell you I speak from experience here. But here is the unbelievably great and freeing news: Our responsibility is to put it in, and God will then use the Word to change us from the inside out. That is the only way true change occurs. Without God's intervention, we are a diseased and dying people. God and God alone can save us and change us.

We need to get the Word of God into our hearts and minds. If our Bibles stay closed for the lack of perfect circumstance, it is not going to happen.

Although this may sound contradictory, we are not passive in this endeavor. We accept the authority of the Word, and through the indwelling of God's Spirit we apply it, bringing our lives into conformity with what the Bible calls us to do. But all this we do only through the power of the Spirit He gives. Surely on our own we could never live in the way God calls for us to live.

What about all the other good influences in our Christian lives? Can't we pick up the Word through the teaching of others? Sure, we may pick up bits and pieces along the way from sermons, devotionals, and the like. However, when we read a devotional and try to apply it, or hear a good point in a sermon and try to work on an area in the absence of a life that is grounded in the Word of God, it is as though we are using a topical antibiotic on a systemic disease. We need a stronger medication that works from the inside out. We're using an antiseptic when we need chemotherapy.

Furthermore, what we pick up along the way from others may not be accurate and we won't see the error unless we have knowledge of the Word itself against which to measure it—a plumb line* if you will.

Dropping the Plumb Line

Just recently I had an internet instant message conversation with a friend who was asking how to evaluate "Christian" books when buying them online from a secular bookseller. "How can I know," she asked "that the book will be what we believe?" I answered that her best bet was to go with a trusted publisher, but the key issue goes way beyond knowing which publishers tend to be "okay." The issue here is one of the plumb line. When we

---

* The plumb line is the symbol of Precept Ministries International.

know the truth, we can hold all other ideas and theories and beliefs up to it and see if they are straight.

In our world today, people look to various sources of authority to help them find their paths in life. I hesitate to say that people use these sources of authority to determine for themselves what is right and wrong, since right and wrong really do not exist in the minds of post-modern American thinkers. Still, people do put stock in each of the following four unreliable sources of authority:

When we know the truth, we can hold all other ideas and theories and beliefs up to it and see if they are straight.

- Culture - What everyone else is doing.
- Tradition - What we've always done.
- Reason - What my mind tells me.
- Feelings - What my emotions tell me.

My husband, dad, and brother-in-law recently finished off our basement. As they roughed in a closet door, my brother-in-law, a former carpenter, did it by eye. Fortunately, he now has a different day job. It didn't look too bad. We could tell it was off a little, but, hey, it's a basement, right? Well, when the real carpenter came to hang the closet doors, guess what happened? That's right, the closet doors wouldn't fit because the wall wasn't plumb; it wasn't even close enough to "make it work." So, instead of just hanging the door, Steve, the professional, had to break into the existing wall to make it straight enough to work. How did he know what straight was? He pulled out a little tool that showed him. He measured the error against the truth.

Just as a carpenter can't "eyeball" a wall to see if it is straight, but rather needs a level or a plumb line, we too need a spiritual plumb line by which to measure. That plumb line is the Word of God. In fact, the only true plumb line in life is the Word of God. But guess what? A dusty Bible on a shelf is worthless; it is like a plumb line that has never been dropped. What good is a plumb line that is not used? Does it give the carpenter any magical guidance in constructing a straight wall? Nope. The level abandoned in the worker's truck is of no value to anyone.

Even if you assent to the fact that the Bible is totally true, and that it is the only true guide for life, if you don't know what is in it, your belief in its veracity is essentially worthless.

Even if you assent to the fact that the Bible is totally true and that it is the only true guide for life, if you don't know what is in it, your belief in its veracity is essentially worthless. *You can't live by principles you don't know.* And while it may seem like a daunting task to get to know what the Bible says, there is no more valuable, rewarding, or life-changing adventure you could ever undertake! So, bag the *Eco-Challenge* this year, tear up your *Survivor* application, and let's get going!

Part Two: The Barriers

Reading the Bible is an intensely personal affair. There are many ways to accomplish a read-through of the Bible. Some do it grudgingly to pass a college requirement; others follow strict schedules with a passage from both the Old and New Testaments every day. Still others try plowing straight through from beginning to end. Different methods work for different people. The goal of this book is not to present a system, per se, but rather to help you identify barriers to reading and thereby help you to remove them; to help you stop making excuses and start making progress. So often our minds simply get "stuck in the mud" and we find that we are crippling ourselves by our limited thinking. We let the enemy tell us that we can't do it and we just take him at his word.

My mind goes to the story of the woman who always cut the end off of the roast before putting it in the oven. One day as she was preparing dinner for the family her daughter asked her, "Mommy, why do you always cut the end off of the roast before you cook it?" Her mom answered, "Well, sweetie, that's what Grandma always did." The girl was not satisfied. Later that evening, when the extended family arrived for dinner, the girl asked her grandma, "Grandma, why did you always cut the end off the roast before cooking it?" Grandma answered, looking over at her mother, the girl's great-grandmother, "I always did it, because that's how Great-Granny always prepared her roasts." The girl looked toward Great-Granny, who laughed and said, "I cut off the end of the roast, because it wouldn't fit in the pan."

For years, I kept "cutting the end off the roast" in my Bible reading. I had developed set ways of thinking that I constantly applied to my Bible reading, thoughts like:

- *If I'm going to read through the Bible, then I need to start at the beginning and read through to the end.*
- *If I'm going to read the Bible, then I have to understand everything that I read right away.*
- *If I'm going to read the Bible, then I have to have "quiet" time and read under perfect conditions.*
- *If I'm going to read through the Bible, then I have to stick to a set reading schedule.*
- *If I'm going to read through the Bible, then I have to muster up the energy to do it by myself–and I just can't. I simply don't have it in me.*

I don't know when exactly I picked up these thoughts, but I operated by them nonetheless and each in its own *way hampered me as I sought to read. They became real barriers to reading through my Bible. Every time I tried to read, I went about it the same way, with the same set of presuppositions, listening to the same lies from the enemy, and every time with the same results . . . failure. I just got stuck. I wanted to read through the Bible, honestly I did, but I felt powerless to accomplish the task. Finally, I started praying that God would give me a relentless desire for His Word. And that is where it all begins, asking God for the desire. As He answered that prayer, and I began reading, God helped me out of the ruts I had been in and revolutionized my reading.*

As you read, please feel free to skim over as needed the barriers and practical points for breaking them. Some will apply to you. Some will not. Don't waste your time on issues that don't apply to your situation. The goal of this book is only to point you to and help you to read another Book, so use this as a reference in whatever way is helpful to you. ***This book will not change your life. The Other will!*** *I guarantee it!*

I have to Read the Bible from Front to Back

How many people do you know who have read Genesis and Exodus more times than they can remember? Maybe you are one of them. I certainly am. For some reason, we in the western culture have this thing about picking up a book, starting on the first page and going straight on through to the end. Not that there's anything wrong with that, particularly if you are reading fiction; it just isn't necessary when you are reading the Bible, a book that is actually a compilation of various shorter writings.

Chances are you already realize from at least one failure that reading from the start of the Bible and trying to go straight through poses an enormous challenge.

Sure, it's the same amount of material regardless of the order in which you read. But, practically speaking, your odds of actually finishing Leviticus and Numbers increase dramatically if you don't try to tackle them in order.

Unlike most books which are arranged strictly chronologically, the Bible has been compiled by general categories. Sure, it starts with the creation of the world, and ends with the new heaven and new earth with Christ the ultimate Victor, certainly giving the casual observer the sense of chronology, but in between the books are generally clumped together more by genre than chronology. We see the Old Testament falling into the general categories of Law, History, Poetry/Wisdom Literature, and Prophecy. In the New Testament we see the Gospels, the Acts of the Apostles, the Epistles (letters), and Prophecy.

So why is reading from the beginning a barrier? Basically, because it sets people up for failure, and failure leads to resignation. We all start off with excitement, thinking we can read straight through the Bible. We try hard. Sometimes we try hard over and over. We fail. We give up. We end up with a scenario that goes something like this:

- *I am going to read through the Bible this year. I know I can do it. I'm starting in Genesis and by next December, I'll be finishing up Revelation.*
- *I can't believe how long Leviticus is. I will never be able to get through this book, much less the entire Bible. I really thought it would be different*

Biblical Genres

OLD TESTAMENT

Law/Books of Moses
Genesis
Exodus
Leviticus
Numbers
Deuteronomy

History
Joshua
Judges
Ruth
I Samuel
II Samuel
I Kings
II Kings
I Chronicles
II Chronicles
Ezra
Nehemiah
Esther

Poetry and Wisdom Literature
Job
Psalms
Proverbs
Ecclesiastes
Song of Solomon

Major Prophets
Isaiah
Jeremiah
Lamentations (of Jeremiah)
Ezekiel
Daniel

Minor Prophets
Hosea
Joel
Amos
Obadiah
Jonah
Micah
Nahum
Habakkuk
Zephaniah
Haggai
Zechariah
Malachi

NEW TESTAMENT

Gospels
Matthew
Mark
Luke
John

History of the Early Church
Acts of the Apostles

Pauline Epistles
Romans
I Corinthians
II Corinthians
Galatians
Ephesians
Philippians
Colossians
I Thessalonians
II Thessalonians
I Timothy
II Timothy
Titus
Philemon

General Epistles
Hebrews
James
I Peter
II Peter
I John
II John
III John
Jude

Prophecy
The Revelation

this time. But I've tried and failed so often, I'll bet I just don't have it in me to do it.

- *You know, I'd love to read through the entire Bible, but I've tried and failed so many times that I just don't believe I can do it. I'll stick to devotionals. They're more on my level. The pastor will teach me what I need to know. I'm just not smart enough or disciplined enough or whatever. . . I just can't do it!*

Satan loves it when we think, for whatever reason, that we can't read our Bibles. *Separated from the Word, we are impotent for the kingdom of God.* And unfortunately, that is exactly where much of the visible church is today. We have failed at reading the Bible from the beginning, so we believe that we don't have the skills to handle the Bible at all.

Break down the barrier! Stop making this excuse! You don't have to read the Bible in order! I know, you may not believe me, but it's true! To help you get started in reading "out of order," here are a few practical tips I've picked up along the way.

Practical Point: ***Try starting with I Samuel***

If you've been a Christian for any length of time at all, chances are pretty good that you have had at least a measure of success in reading some New Testament books. It's the Old Testament that seems like the highest mountain to scale. After all, it's about three times as long as the New

Testament, it has books like Leviticus and Ezekiel and Job, and the longest chapter in the Old Testament (Psalm 119) is longer by itself than several of the New Testament *books*! So, in my estimation, any attempt at reading through the Bible needs to start with a successful dip in the Old Testament. To be perfectly honest, I tend to be a person who likes to get the hardest stuff out of the way first so I can cruise home with material that's a little easier, but I don't recommend that approach with the Old Testament.

In reading the Old Testament, I've found I Samuel a wonderful place to start. It reads like a story and is not nearly as long as the books of the Law. Beginning with the story of Hannah, the mother of the prophet Samuel as she cries out to God for a son, the book of I Samuel also tells the story of Saul, the first King of Israel, of David and Goliath, and of the continual pursuit of David by Saul. It concludes with the death of Saul, setting the reader up for a continued trip into II Samuel. This narrative then continues right into I and II Kings.

At the end of II Kings, the people go into captivity, which led me in my reading to the books of Jeremiah and Lamentations that have to do with the Babylonian captivity.

Practical Point: ***Remember that the Old Testament is filled with stories***

Indulge me here for one more quick point on the Old Testament in general. Have you picked up a children's

Bible anytime recently? If so, what have you seen? That's right, a heavy helping of stories from the Old Testament. Sure, you'll find stories about Jesus, too, and a few about Paul. But you'll have tons of Old Testament *stories*! I don't use the word *story* here in the sense of something fictitious, but to help you connect with the fact that much of the Old Testament is really captivating reading.

When brought to the appropriate level, it holds the attention of kids—and they can be some of the toughest critics out there! It is also understandable to kids, which means you can get it too!

Practical Point: ***Even if you're tempted, don't start in Genesis***

Another day, another time . . . try it then. Try starting in Genesis when you have already successfully made your way through the entire Bible more than once. Don't get me wrong, Genesis is great reading, it is just *so* towards the front of the book and it is so long (50 chapters).

The problem is that you'll be reading for a long time before you really sense that you are making progress. If you start further in, you'll feel like you're making progress faster and be more inclined to keep going.

The other problem with starting in Genesis is that even if you do make it through this book in a relatively timely fashion, you'll be tempted to continue on in a linear fashion and will soon find out how hard it is to read the end of Exodus, all of Leviticus, and the beginning of

Numbers consecutively. And even if you do make it through those and cruise on towards the "easy-reading" historical books, you will eventually hit the wall known as *Isaiahjeremiahlamentationsezekiel.*

Sure, Lamentations is only five chapters long, but have you done a page count on the other three lately? They're good when they're taken in portions, but try to swallow them whole and you'll choke. At least I still do. Maybe the "giants" can ingest those in succession, but for the rest of us, I suggest smaller portions.

One exception here: If you do not have any background in the stories of the Bible from Sunday School experiences or other teaching and do not know the basic stories of Creation, Noah, Abraham, Isaac, Jacob, and Joseph then you need to start in Genesis. Don't continue in order after that, but do read Genesis first. After that, you might want to try I Samuel or one of the Gospels (Matthew, Mark, Luke, or John).

Practical Point: ***Don't think you can ignore the Old Testament***

If you've been a Christian for awhile and have never read the Old Testament, you may have reasoned to yourself that because we have a new covenant in Jesus Christ, we really don't need to read what was in the old covenant. As rationalizations go, it sounds pretty good. And given a choice between the two, certainly, you'd have to go with the New Testament. The thing is, though, we can never, ever get a grasp on how great the new covenant is without first understanding the old covenant. Much of the New Testament will remain a closed book to you, because you won't understand the foundations and you won't have a full understanding of God.

I run into students all the time who get frustrated reading their New Testaments largely, I believe, because they don't have the Old Testament foundation on which the New Testament rests. God gave us the entire Bible for a reason; we need to be about the business of reading all of it.

Not only that, the New Testament tells us that the Old Testament provides us examples, both good and bad, about how we should live. In the first letter to the Corinthians, the Apostle Paul says in chapter 10 verse 6, "Now these things happened as examples for us, so that we would not crave evil things as they also craved." He goes on in verses 11–12 to say, "Now these things happened to them as an example, and they were written for our instruction, upon whom the ends of the ages have come. Therefore let him who thinks he stands take heed that he does not fall."

Practical Point: ***Make good use of your Table of Contents***

Complex systems work for some people. They certainly don't work for me. I recently talked to a woman in a

Scripture reading program with daily readings from both the Old and New Testaments. She loves it, and it has helped guide her through the Bible. Great! For most of us, though, the more complex the system, the less chance we'll make it, just based on the "I missed a day" principle if nothing else.

Ever notice how hard it is to catch up when you miss a day on a schedule . . . *any* schedule? If the washing machine doesn't run when it's supposed to, or the dishes slide by for one meal without being dealt with, the resulting problem is more than the sum of its parts. Same thing when you're dealing with a strict Bible reading schedule. When you miss a day, the tendency is to want to do the catch up every time. Instead of "having" to read three chapters in a day, all of a sudden you could be looking at six, nine, twelve, or worse.

Then we have the guilt of looking at what we *haven't* done. "I should be *there* by now, but I'm only *here*." In my estimation, complex schedules move us squarely into the academic realm. When my eyes see the word "schedule," my soul sees the word "syllabus," and the relational aspect of the activity diminishes.

Practical Point: ***Use mind games to your benefit***

Success tends to breed more success, and failure tends to breed more failure. We all know this from just living our lives and watching the lives of others. Take school, for example. Scoring well on a test tends to buoy up a student and spur him or her on to greater things. Once you've achieved a 98% on a test, you know you've got the right stuff and can pull it off again. The second, third, and fourth times are always easier, because you have the confidence to succeed. Likewise, when you score a 40% after having exerted yourself, it is much harder to gain the courage to try again.

For this reason, it is important to see yourself making progress toward your goal; small successes along the way can help you gain serious momentum. Think with me for a moment about the typical path for reading the Bible, bearing in mind that when you look at that Table of Contents you're staring at a list of 66 entries. If you start at Genesis and proceed forward, you have a good 90 chapters in the first two books—generally good reading here, but the check marks aren't exactly flying onto the page. So by the time you hit the Leviticus/Numbers wall, you don't have much in the way of visual "success" to look at in your Table of Contents. Having read Genesis and Exodus, you would have covered a great deal of ground, but you will likely feel less "on a roll" than if you knock off a few of the smaller books first.

A "spiritual" way of doing things? Maybe not. But it has worked for me. Remember, we're not looking here to be super spiritual. We are not trying to change ourselves. We're just putting the material in and letting God do the work from the inside out.

***Practical Point:* Read Epistles in their entirety**

I can't stress this one enough. An epistle is a letter. How do you read a letter? I'm guessing that you don't do it in more than one sitting. "Okay, three paragraphs today, three tomorrow, and three on Friday." It just doesn't happen that way, does it? It shouldn't happen that way with epistles either.

So many of us have become 5-minute devotional Christians that we really don't know how to sit down and digest a larger portion of Scripture or how to interact and read for more than ten or fifteen minutes at a time tops! The Epistles are a great place to break the "I'll read one chapter today" habit. Sure, one chapter a day is better than no chapters, but that type of reading can cause such problems because we tend to lose context. And it is in context that we understand what the author is really saying. So use the Epistles as a training ground for observing context and learning to sit and read for increasing periods of time.

You'll find all of the Epistles located in the New Testament. They were letters written to first century churches after Christ had ascended to heaven. Most of them, the Pauline Epistles, were written by the Apostle Paul. The name of the book or epistle is taken from the name of the recipients. The Pauline corpus includes the following: Romans, I and II Corinthians, Galatians, Ephesians, Philippians, Colossians, I and II Thessalonians, I and II Timothy, Titus, and Philemon.

The other grouping of epistles that you'll find are termed the General Epistles. They include Hebrews, James, I and II Peter, I, II, and III John, and Jude. The General Epistles generally bear the name of the author as the book title, the Epistle to the Hebrews being the exception. Although there is much speculation as to whom the author of Hebrews may be, internal evidence almost certainly rules out the Apostle Paul.

Practical Point: ***Read Minor Prophets in their entirety***

As with the Epistles, you're better off reading the Minor Prophets in one sitting. Each are relatively short books, hence, the term "minor." The Minor Prophets are Hosea, Joel, Amos, Obadiah, Jonah, Micah, Nahum, Habakkuk, Zephaniah, Haggai, Zechariah, and Malachi. The books range in length from one chapter to fourteen. When reading the Prophets, it is essential that you ask, at the very least, these two basic questions to gain a basic understanding of the book:

Who is it written to?

The answer will usually be Israel (Northern Kingdom) or Judah (Southern Kingdom).

When was it written?

The answer you are looking for is before or after the nation has been conquered. Has the nation already been conquered due to judgment, or is the book looking forward to and predicting coming judgment?

If you don't have at least a basic understanding of the history of Israel, you'll find it helpful to read some of the historical books before moving into the Prophets. If, however, you have the basic gist of the Divided Kingdom and the subsequent captivities, feel free to zip through the Minor Prophets early on and finish what looks like in the Table of Contents about a quarter of the Old Testament.

Sidebar History Lesson

In the Old Testament we hear, among other things, the story of the people of Israel. But sometimes we hear the name Judah thrown in, or references to Jerusalem or Samaria. If you've got all these names under control, skip this sidebar; if you're not sure how they all fit together, read on!

FAMILY TREE

The people of Israel take their name from the grandson of Abraham, who we usually hear referred to as Jacob. God, however, renames him Israel, and from this comes the name of the Jewish people–Israel.

DEFINITIONS

ISRAEL - The name given to Jacob by God. Later becomes the name of the nation descended from him. Eventually, Israel becomes a divided nation, with 2 of the 12 tribes remaining with Rehoboam, the son of Solomon, while the other 10 tribes follow Jeroboam. These 10 tribes retain the name Israel. The capital of Israel was Samaria. It is also referred to as the Northern Kingdom. All of the kings of the North were evil; some more, some less. Israel was captured in 722 BC by Assyria. Most of the inhabitants were deported and scattered; those remaining intermarried with other people groups who were brought into Israel by Assyria.

JUDAH - Judah was one of the sons of Jacob (Israel). Judah was originally one of the 12 tribes of Israel. After the division of the kingdom, however, it was used to refer to the two tribes that remained with Rehoboam, the son of Solomon, while the other 10 tribes followed Jeroboam. The capital of Judah was Jerusalem. It is also referred to as the Southern Kingdom. In the Southern Kingdom, the kings were a mixed bag–some good, some bad, some very bad. Judah was captured in 586 BC by Babylon. The inhabitants were taken into captivity in Babylon for 70 years and then were allowed to return to their land.

EPHRAIM - While the Northern Kingdom is usually referred to as Israel, it is occasionally called Ephraim. This is not just an attempt to confuse you. Rather, the name is taken from the largest tribe in the Northern Kingdom.

SAMARIA - Samaria was the capital of Israel, the Northern Kingdom of 10 tribes that followed non-Davidic kings.

JERUSALEM - Jerusalem was the capital of Judah, the Southern Kingdom of 2 tribes that followed the Davidic kings.

UNITED KINGDOM - Israel was a United Kingdom of 12 tribes under the leadership first of Saul, and then of David and his son, Solomon.

DIVIDED KINGDOM - Solomon's son, Rehoboam, ticked people off big time–so much so that 10 of the tribes took off to follow a man named Jeroboam.

NORTHERN KINGDOM - Ten northern tribes ruled by non-Davidic kings. Also referred to as Israel. The capital was Samaria.

SOUTHERN KINGDOM - Two southern tribes ruled by the Davidic line of kings. Comprised of the tribes of Judah and Benjamin, the Southern Kingdom is referred to simply as "Judah." The capital of the Southern Kingdom was Jerusalem.

Practical Point: ***Read Hebrews and Leviticus in succession***

I see your eyebrows going up. Leviticus by itself can be a tough read; truth be told, so can Hebrews. However, if you have just finished the book of Hebrews, which focuses on Jesus as our Great High Priest, you will find that Leviticus is very helpful in understanding what is going on in Hebrews and vice versa. All of a sudden, with a reference point of Christ, everything makes a little more sense.

Practical Point: ***Read Leviticus in three sittings tops; try to do it in one***

I had a great childhood, for the most part. I always knew without a doubt that my parents loved me, but . . . they made me eat vegetables. To this day I can taste in my mind the cold beets, feel the squish of the cold green beans, and vividly recall the gagging sensation as I tried to swallow them as close to whole as possible with a swig of milk that had once been cold. Every day my Dad would say, "Pam, if you'll just eat them while they're warm, and get it over with, it won't be so bad." And every day I would dawdle at the dinner table, stretching those veggies out until they nearly molded on my plate in front of me.

All this to say, for me, reading through Leviticus a chapter a day is like trying to swallow cold vegetables whole as Leviticus is an entire book of dos and don'ts for ancient Israel. (I saw that yawn.) Are there lessons to be learned in Leviticus? Absolutely. Will I see these lessons the first time I read it? Maybe not. Will it be as fun to read as the Gospel of John? No. Regardless of what you seem to "get out of it" the first time through, even Leviticus will help you to understand the whole context of the Bible. It will help you to see how high and extensive the standards of God are and how impossible it is to be a "law-keeper." It will help you to understand the seriousness of sin and the holiness of God.

Is Leviticus a place to stop and study deeply? Eventually. But on a first trip through the Bible, I would suggest clearing an hour and swallowing whole. This time through, we want to become familiar with the general context of the Bible, the broad sweeping strokes on the canvas, so that when we go back to study in-depth we have a better understanding of the whole. Leviticus is a place that can slow you down; don't let it this time.

Practical Point: When you're having a hard time reading, stick to historical books or the Gospels

Sometimes reading the Bible just gets to be hard. Maybe you're behind at work, or the kids are super owly, or you'd do anything just to sit and watch TV for awhile. Whether it's spiritual warfare or just the circumstances of life, there will be times when opening your Bible is tough. That's when it's the most important to "just do it." You don't want to get into martyr mode, however. You know what I mean, "Oh, my favorite television show is on, but I guess I'll just sit here and read Leviticus instead and see how (sigh) I can apply it to my life today." If you're struggling, try to sit for awhile in the books that are easier to read. In general, the historical books and the Gospels tend to read like stories.

The Gospels (Matthew, Mark, Luke, and John) open up the New Testament. The first three, Matthew, Mark, and Luke are often referred to as the Synoptic Gospels because they tell the stories of Jesus in a similar fashion and have some overlapping accounts. Why three? Three different audiences. Matthew wrote to a primarily Jewish audience, Mark to Romans, and Luke, the physician, wrote to a Greek audience. The Gospel of John takes a slightly different approach to the presentation of Jesus, being written around seven major signs Jesus performed with the specific purpose that the readers might "believe that Jesus is the Christ, the Son of God; and that believing you may have life in His name" (John 20:31b).

Practical Point: When you're feeling "behind," rip off a few Minor Prophets or Epistles in a single sitting

I realize this probably sounds really unspiritual. (Sorry, I'm still a work in progress!) But realize we don't have to be in a super spiritual mood for God to work in our hearts and our minds. Sometimes we just need that boost of checking off a few books. And with twelve Minor Prophets ranging in length from one chapter (Obadiah) to fourteen (Hosea and Zechariah), the Minor Prophets are a place you can feel like you're really making some progress.

As I mentioned earlier, though, don't dive into these books without first reading some of the historical books unless you have a reasonable understanding of the history of Israel.

***Practical Point:* Hit the Major Prophets (Isaiah, Jeremiah, Ezekiel), Leviticus, and Numbers when you are "on a roll," but make sure you knock off at least one Major Prophet relatively early in the year**

Some of you may have been stopped by the fact that I didn't include Daniel when I referred to the Major Prophets. While Daniel is usually lumped in with the majors, it is in fact a much shorter book and immanently more readable. You could easily park yourself and polish it off in one enjoyable sitting.

The big three, on the other hand, are all in the 50-chapter range and although there's much great stuff packed in them, the Prophets tend to be tougher to grasp on a first trip through the Bible than some of the other material. Hence, while you will find some treasures in the majors even without much background (for example, Isaiah 53, the descriptions of God in Ezekiel, etc.), some of the material will leave you scratching your head . . . and that's okay . . . for now. Remember, this is the first time you're reading through the Bible. You're looking for the big picture, the broad strokes, the context of how it all fits together. Details are important, but many of them will come later.

Whatever you do, don't be afraid of the Prophets. When you're ready, jump in and start to swim. I remember being fascinated the first time I read Jeremiah. Did I understand it all? Not even close. But I was struck by the characterization of Israel, by their stiff-necked manner and unrepentant heart and I came to a better understanding of why God was disciplining them. It wasn't for one bad choice they made. It was for bad choice after bad choice after bad choice. After my "indignant" phase with Israel, I also realized how much like them I often tend to be . . . and I have the benefit of the indwelling Holy Spirit, which they did not have. Let's just say it makes you think.

Practical Point: ***Pay attention to the details (genealogies, etc.), but don't bog down in them now***

If you have to skim a bit on genealogies, Levitical laws, the beginning of the book of Numbers, or the end of Ezekiel, don't beat yourself up about it. Genealogies did nothing for me the first couple of times I read through the Bible and they probably won't do anything for you either. The funny thing is, though, the more I have come to grasp the whole of the Bible (and I still have a *long* ways to go), the more even the seemingly "boring" things have come into focus. Rahab, the prostitute, is in the line of Jesus—interesting. How about the prayer of

Jabez squashed right there in the thick of the Chronicles? There's a worthwhile little gem.

If you happen to be a perfectionist, this may send you into a bit of a craze. After all, if you haven't really read everything, you haven't read everything. My advice: Loosen up! I know, I know, easier said than done, but just for fun give it a whirl. If you feel *that* guilty, next time through you can memorize the genealogies!

Practical Point: Try to ignore the chapter breaks

The chapter and verse breaks are not inspired. And as helpful as they are in navigating the Bible, they get in the way when we read causing us to stop and start like a car on an urban road. Learning to ignore the chapter breaks will cause your reading to be more like an uninterrupted ride through Montana. Additionally, as you read, you'll find several places where chapter and verse breaks actually detract from meaning by grouping content away from its natural context.

Practical Point: Stay away from the footnotes

Footnotes are well meaning helps, but you need to stay away from them as much as possible. They are one man's view of the text you are reading. If you don't understand something, you need to go back and look at the *context*, not the footnotes. If you hang out in the footnotes, you'll be inadvertently buying into a theological school of thought rather than searching the Scriptures for yourself and allowing the Holy Spirit to be your teacher.

Are they helpful? Sure, sometimes. Same thing with commentaries. They can be valuable tools after you have done the digging for yourself.

Practical Point: Read the Psalms and Proverbs concurrently with something else

Chances are you'll love reading the Psalms and Proverbs, provided you don't try to read straight through. I highly suggest reading both of the books of poetry concurrently with something else. Sure, you can read through five or six Psalms in one sitting and learn from them how to worship. If you try to read 20 or 30 at a time, though, you'll just plain overdose. The Psalms are words that really do need to be meditated upon. Don't rush, let them soak into your soul as you read. Pick out a favorite, memorize it, and let the Holy Spirit teach you how to worship through it.

At the same time, however, you need to realize that the Psalms total 150. That means at a rate of one Psalm a day, it would take you nearly a half a year to get through this book. This is fine if you're also reading somewhere else at the same time, and you happen to be a plodder. Sprinters (like myself) will go crazy at a Psalm a day pace. Better for us to read five to ten a day and feel great about our "chapter volume" for a bit.

The Proverbs, on the other hand, will give you good guidelines for life; short, quick little sayings that generally prove to be true if carried out. Again, they are best taken in a chapter or two a day. Otherwise, due to the brevity of the sayings, they will all simply run together in your mind. One of the bigger mistakes many people make when reading the Proverbs is believing that they are actual promises of God to them. They simply are not. Yes, the Bible does contain many promises; they just are not found in the book of Proverbs. Proverbs, as said before, are life principles, which generally hold true. Important? Yes. Helpful? Absolutely. Just don't get your pants in a pinch if you think God is breaking His promises when you see a proverb not holding true.

By the way, there are 31 chapters in the book of Proverbs, which makes it a great one chapter a day read to go along with something else.

Practical Point: ***Don't make someone else reinvent the wheel***

As you read, you are sure to discover some helpful techniques of your own for reading through the Bible. You will also discover areas that are particularly challenging for you. Jot these down on the next page so that you can pass your tips on to others and remember them for yourself another time through. No sense in reinventing the wheel. Share what you have learned to spur someone else on in the faith!

Techniques that have worked for me:

1. ______________________________

2. ______________________________

3. ______________________________

4. ______________________________

5. ______________________________

6. ______________________________

7. ______________________________

8. ______________________________

9. ______________________________

10. ______________________________

Areas of difficulty that I have found in reading through the Bible:

1. ______________________________

2. ______________________________

3. ______________________________

4. ______________________________

5. ______________________________

6. ______________________________

7. ______________________________

8. ______________________________

9. ______________________________

10. ______________________________

I Have to Understand Everything I Read Right Away

Are you the kind of person who's bothered when you don't understand something? I sure am. Drives me nuts. But I'm getting used to it. And if you want to make it through the Bible, you need to also. Don't misunderstand here. It is important to study deeply and to learn to handle accurately the Word of God as Paul tells us in his second letter to Timothy (2:15). That is imperative for disciples of Jesus Christ.

One of the key principles of accurately handling the Word of God, however, has to do with taking material in context. Context is king in matters of interpreting the Word of God. Thus, we need to *read broadly* and *study deeply,* because while the Bible is made up of 66 smaller books, it is still God's Word to man and the context of the whole helps us greatly in understanding individual parts.

So the first time you read through the Bible, don't get unduly concerned when something doesn't seem to click. Don't try to solve the timing of the rapture or become disheartened if you leave the Prophets with more questions than you have answers. Realize that the more you read, the more you will "get it." The more context you have (i.e., the more Bible reading you have done, whether or not you have "gotten" it all), the easier it will be to study deeply and to put the pieces together.

. . . we need to read broadly and study deeply . . .

The converse, I believe, is also true. It is much harder to study deeply when you don't have a degree of working knowledge of the entire corpus of Scripture. Without a strong knowledge of the context of the Bible, your vulnerability level to heresy increases dramatically. Does that really matter? Of course it does, because the most effective lies are those that are mixed thoroughly with large doses of truth.

Realize here, too, that while some would like you to believe that studying the Bible is just this side of "rocket science." It simply is not. The Bible is God's Word to man and its message is within the grasp of all. Just because some people read the Old Testament in Hebrew and can split apart New Testament Greek words doesn't mean that you, by comparison, are a second class Christian. In fact, at times those parsing Greek verbs find they can't see the forest for the trees. In order to study the Bible, you don't need to know the meaning of exegesis or hermeneutics; eschatology or soteriology–not that they aren't fun 50¢ words to carry around in your pocket! What you need is a heart open to God's working and the diligence to continue seeking Him.

This barrier presents a major problem because it either prevents people from ever attempting to read the Bible, or failing to understand everything they give up– and that failure becomes an even stronger barrier to future study.

Practical Point: Understand and value the importance of context

Context is king in reading and studying the Bible. If you get nothing else out of this book, this is the point you need to get: *context is king*. Without context, it is possible to make the Bible say almost anything, to preach or teach anything you choose. Everything becomes relative; everything is gray just like our world today. In truth, nothing can be understood out of context. Therefore, studying deeply without context is next to impossible unless you are relying on someone else to point you to where similar topics come up; while helpful, you will want to eventually learn to go beyond that.

***Practical Point:* Agree with yourself that reading through the Bible will not be a one-time event**

Choosing that you will be a lifelong reader of the Bible is the single most powerful way to break through this barrier. Simply resolve together with God that reading through the Bible will *not* be a one-time "check-it-off-my-life-goal-list" kind of activity. Honestly, the minute you determine to continue to read the Word, the pressure for immediate and total understanding vanishes.

Sure, if you're that "type" (and I speak as one who is), having some questions will eventually spur you on to more study, and that's great. That's what should happen. That's what *needs* to happen. The point here is to keep the questions from totally derailing you as you seek to gain context. You are not ignoring questions; you are taking the first step towards answering them by gaining the additional information of context and extended context.

Think for a moment of a child coming to his parent complaining that his sister hit him. The parent most certainly has questions. Where were you? What were you doing? Did she hit you for a reason? Did you do something to provoke her? Was she just being mean? Now any thinking adult realizes that before any punishment is doled out, questions need to be answered. Not only this, but questions need to be answered from a variety of sources to determine the whole story. What the parent needs is context. Little Jimmy is only going to give part of the story. Mom and Dad need the sister's story: they need to hear from any other eyewitnesses what was going on. They need context.

The great thing about the Bible is that it always provides context. First, it provides the context of the book in which material appears, and then the context of the whole Bible. Since Scripture interprets Scripture, you'll find that difficult passages in certain areas will clear dramatically when you read other parts of Scripture. But you have to be reading the whole thing to be able to use this principle effectively.

Practical Point: ***Get rid of the pencil***

Okay. Now I know I've offended some people. After all, telling a "pencil reader" to abandon the lead is like telling a chain smoker to go cold turkey, maybe worse. I speak here as Queen of the Pencil Readers. Understand I am not saying never read the Bible with a pencil. I do it all the time, but the first time I made it through, I didn't. I do suggest, however, if this is your first time reading through the Bible, drop the pencil with the understanding that you can underline all you want the next time through; and the time after that; and the time after that.

Why? *By setting down the pencil, we begin to interact with the Word as a book instead of an assignment.* Do you read novels with a pencil? Do you use a highlighter when you pick up the magazine?

The key here is two-fold. First, we need to learn to enjoy reading the Bible, to have it be a natural "pick up." Second, we need to read the first time for the overall message to start to see how everything holds together. The more we read, the clearer everything becomes, but if we get so bogged down in the minutia the first time around, the odds that we'll make it back through a second, third, or fourth time diminish.

So, don't knock it until you try it. Drop the pencil and see if your attitude towards reading changes like mine did. No guarantees here, but give it a try.

Actually, right now I'm reading through the New American Standard Bible on my laptop computer and using the Precept Ministries marking tools to mark key words and phrases with different colors and symbols . . . how cool is that?! Okay, maybe I'm weird, but it gives me a thrill!

Practical Point: ***Lose the overly high emotional expectations***

The earth won't move every time you read the Bible. Sometimes it will, but don't count on it every day. Some days God will seem so near that you'll hardly be able to comprehend it. Other days He'll seem distant. Just keep going. Keep putting the Word in and letting Him work on the person He wants you to become.

Over time you will find God making changes in you, making you more and more like Jesus. Realize, this may be imperceptible to you at the start, but chances are others around you will begin to notice a change and all of a sudden you'll realize that things that used to be very important to you are not so much any more, and other things are beginning to take their places.

We get so hung up on our emotions; we want goosebumps and a certain feeling in the pit of our stomachs, but that is not what Christianity is about. It is about a confidence and hope in God; it is about a sound mind and a clean heart, not bumpy skin and warm intestines.

***Practical Point:* Get it in and trust God to use it**

I can't stress this one enough, particularly if you are an I-have-to-understand-everything type of person. If you are truly a child of God and seek Him through His Word, God will use that Word to affect radical change in your life. Let me say that again, *God* will use that Word to affect radical change in your life. This is a biggie. You obey by seeking Him, but you must realize that only He can change you; only He can give you understanding. That being the case, it is imperative that we put the Word in and allow Him to work.

***Practical Point:* Read broadly**

The Bible can be a tough book to grasp. Although authored by God whose message is consistent, the Bible was at the same time written through various human "authors." Thus, while the message is consistent throughout, different human authors have different styles and stress different concepts.

All this to say, as you study deeply, the broad reading you do will make more sense because you are coming to understand in a more thorough way the concepts of the Bible. At the same time, the more broadly you read, the more sense you will be able to make of individual passages because you will have better understanding of the larger context.

I learned this concept my freshman year in college from our college chaplin whose walk matched his talk. It has stuck with me over the years. I love it because it is easy to remember and provides a balance that is needed, but sometimes difficult to maintain when studying the Bible.

***Practical Point:* Join a Bible study where you will learn to study deeply**

Study the Bible deeply with a heart that is seeking God, and God will change your life. Reading through the Bible will help you to get the big picture; it will help you with context; it will help you see how things hang together. It helps us to hear God, and God uses it in our lives to strengthen each of our relationships with Him.

It is His Word, and His Words truly are life to us. I can't even find words to express the importance of seeking to digest the full counsel of God. But in order to digest fully the Word of God, we need to learn how to be good students of the Word, as well. As Paul says in II Timothy 2:15, we need to learn to accurately handle the Word of truth. A solid biblically-based inductive study will help you in doing just this.

For some people, study is just not a good word. It is, nonetheless, vital in a growing relationship with God. A good study will help you learn to ask the right questions of the text, such as:

- Who wrote the text?
- To whom was it written?
- Why was it written?
- When was it written?
- What are the key words in the text?
- What is the theme of the book?
- What is the theme of the individual chapters?

A good study will help you learn how to do word studies to find out what nuances specific words had in their original language (Greek for the NT, Hebrew for most of the OT). No, you don't have to learn Greek and Hebrew to make use of the study tools! (See Appendix B for a listing of Greek/Hebrew study tools.) A good study will also help you to see texts in their near and greater context, and to let Scripture interpret itself. A good Bible study will not ask, "What does this mean to you?" but rather, it will help you determine what the text meant to the original hearers and then, based on that, how it can apply in our lives today. A Precept Ministries Bible study, for example, will teach you to ask, "Now that I've studied, how does understanding the meaning of the text apply to me?" Learning to study helps to keep us from reading our own views into the text.

An excellent book on this topic is Kay Arthur's *How to Study Your Bible.** It takes you step by step through the inductive study method, which will help you to learn to dig out the truths of God's Word for yourself. My favorite for in-depth Bible study is Precept Ministries International, but there are many solid Bible studies out there these days. I hear good things about Bible Study Fellowship also know as BSF (which also has a very strong children's program) and the Beth Moore studies, just to name a couple. (See Appendix C for further information.)

Practical Point: **Find a Paul**

What, you ask, is a "Paul?" A "Paul" is a mentor in the faith (someone who disciples to put it in biblical terms), a person who is more spiritually mature than yourself who can help you in your spiritual growth and understanding of Scripture. While we'll deal with the mentoring concept in greater depth later in this book, you need to know that a

---

* *How to Study Your Bible* by Kay Arthur, Harvest House Publishers: Eugene, Oregon, 1994.

mentor can help you discern what in the Bible is most important to understand fully. Don't have a grasp on the humanity and deity of Jesus? That's a problem. Having trouble with sequencing all of the Old Testament prophecy and the eschatology of the New Testament? A good mentor will be able to help clear up some of the cloudy issues and point you in the direction of study that is going to be of most help to you in your spiritual walk.

The ultimate goal is to handle accurately the Word of truth on your own, but along the way, a mentor can be a tremendous help. A good mentor will also be helpful in calling you to task on whether or not you are applying and living out what you are reading and studying.

A good mentor will also be able to encourage you when the going gets tough. And it will get tough at times because we are in a war. Our enemy will not take our getting serious with God sitting down. I don't say this to scare you. I say this to remind you, because forewarned is forearmed.

Practical Point:* *Learn to be an active reader

While we're not trying to answer every question the first time through, that doesn't preclude interacting vigorously with the text and asking questions of it as you read. "Who is the writer? Why is he writing? To whom is the book addressed? Why was it written?" In order to catch what is going on, we need to train ourselves to ask questions of the text in the course of our reading to help us to see the whole picture. Just think back to the journalistic 5 Ws and the H to help you as you read:

- Who is writing? Who is being written to?
- What is he trying to say?
- Where was it going? From where was it written?
- Why did the author write?
- When was the book written?
- Are there any specific "How" questions that the text answers?

Eventually, you'll answer these questions on paper or computer as you start studying the text deeply, but for now, answer them in your head as you go along. Be a journalist; ask the questions, get the answers!

Practical Point: ***Avoid the temptation to Spiritualize***

Have you ever sat in a "Bible study" (and, yes, the quotation marks are deliberate) where everyone in the group takes a turn telling what a particular passage means to them? I hope you haven't, but I'm guessing at some point you have. This is one way in which we do not handle accurately the Word of truth.

Yes, the Bible speaks to us today, but that speaking must come out of an understanding of what the text said to its original hearers. What it means must come out of what it meant. And for that, sorry to be so repetitive, we need context and study.

Practical Point: ***Avoid the temptation to Naturalize***

When we naturalize the Bible, we disallow anything that is not empirical. By empirical I mean anything that cannot be seen, measured, touched, felt, examined, or proved. According to a naturalistic view, miracles could not have happened because they do not fit the way that we *know* the world operates. People do not rise from the dead. Therefore, accordingly, Jesus could not have been raised from the dead, neither could He have raised others from the dead. Furthermore, we all know that those of flesh and blood cannot walk on water unless it has been significantly below 32 degrees Fahrenheit. Five loaves of bread and two fish cannot feed 5,000 men, to say nothing of their dates.

Now, while many would not think of viewing the New Testament in a naturalistic way, the Old Testament is quite another story. It is not uncommon to find people who accept the miracles of Jesus, but can't bring themselves to believe that a big fish swallowed a little man named Jonah. Similarly, they can accept Jesus as God, but can't accept that God may actually have made the earth in six days like He says.

Certainly, the Bible uses figurative language at times; the Psalms, Revelation, and the Prophets are some examples. And when figurative language is used, we need to interpret the material in the manner that the author intended. We can't, however, force the term "figurative" language or "allegory" on people or events that Jesus spoke of as being the real thing. If you're feeling disagreeable here, just consider what I'm saying, mark your margin and move on.

Practical Point: *Avoid the temptation to Dogmatize*

If you grew up in the church you probably struggle with this problem to some degree whether or not you realize it. Dogmatizing makes the Bible agree with a view that is already held, whether or not the original view is truly scriptural. For example, you will approach the Bible differently if you believe in predestination as opposed to the free will of man. If you think you can lose your salvation, you will approach passages differently than if you believe that your salvation is eternally secure.

Your church may have pet views on the rapture of the church, or baptism, or any one of a number of things. Because of the views that surround us and our own preconceived ideas, the tendency to read into the Bible what we think it says can become very great. We all have presuppositions. We need to be aware of them and keep them in check as we come to the Bible. The more we allow the Bible to speak for itself and to interpret itself, the better off we will be.

Furthermore, choosing between two opposing views or dogmas may put us on a wrong path. Some combined biblical truths (such as the sovereignty of God and the free will of man) may not make sense to us, but they do to God. By faith I accept both, let God solve the apparent dilemma, and simply move on in my study of the Bible. We can easily get hung up on some of these "difficulties" and get sidetracked from much more important things.

My father-in-law, who is a long-time pastor, explains it this way, "We read the Bible like we eat fish. When we come upon a bone, we just lift it out, lay it aside, and go on eating. When we come upon a 'bone' in Scripture we do the same, lay it aside and go on reading. I may find the answer further on in my study or I may simply have to leave it with God. After all, He is omniscient and I am not. The fact that I cannot understand some of these apparent clashes of truth helps me to accept the fact that God is far greater than I am and He is worthy of my trust."

You will also find that the more you read (if you are reading with an open mind), the less you will find yourself holding onto the dogma of men. When we don't know the truth for ourselves, we often cling to the dogmas of men because we long for something that is true and stable. We'll fight for positions that we really know nothing about because we have a need for security and stability. When you get into the Word of God, though, you find the source of truth, and the dogmas of man no longer become so important. As Jesus says in the Gospel of John (8:32), "and you will know the truth, and the truth will make you free."

***Practical Point:* Start practicing your hermeneutical leaps**

Okay, I know I said you didn't have to know what hermeneutics and exegesis are, but you do need to understand the English concepts that they stand for. Hermeneutics is just a fancy word that means the art and science of interpreting Scripture. It involves two basic steps:

- Drawing out what the text meant to its original hearers (also called exegesis, from the Greek word, meaning "to draw out").
- Applying the text today based on what it originally meant.

Realize that while the text of Scripture can be applied in more than one way, valid application must come out of what the text meant to its original hearers in their context.

Hermeneutical Leap

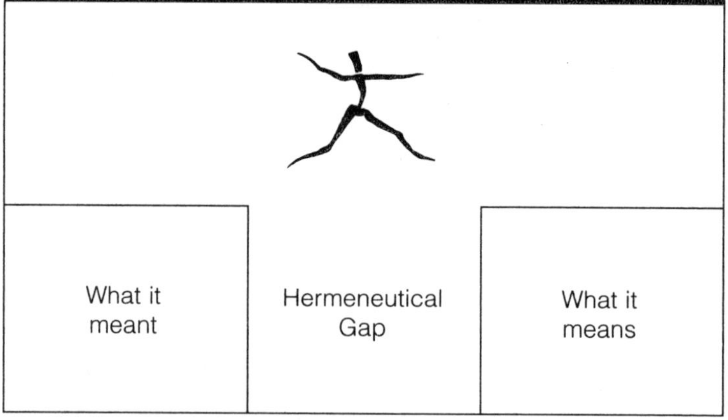

We need to understand what the biblical text meant to its original hearers before we can make application to our lives today.

Practical Point: ***Apply the clear teaching and live in the light of it***

If we're honest, it is not the 1% or 5% or even 10% of the Bible that we don't understand that poses the problem for us; it is the 99%, 95%, or 90% that we *do* understand. Sure, we can all come up with a few perplexing scriptural references that give us fits, but how much would alternate interpretations actually affect the way we live our lives? Probably not at all.

Conversely, how differently would the visible church today look if people were into the Word of God and being transformed from the inside out into people who love the brethren, who pursue peace with all men, who let their lights shine, who walk in the light, who hold marriage in honor, who are not shackled by the love of money or by the fear of death . . . are you getting my point here?

How different would the church at large look if we followed Paul's instructions to Titus on how older men, older women, younger women, and young men should live?

Practical Point: ***Always interpret unclear teaching in light of clear teaching, not vice versa***

I'll never forget the first time that I had to read through the book of Romans. I was a grade schooler and had to read the book to pass a couple of sections in my Awana Clubs handbook. I was cruising right along, until I ran into Romans 9 like a box of bricks in the middle of a clear highway. I was lying on the red-carpeted floor of our family room, and all of a sudden I saw what I perceived to be a different God in the pages of Scripture than the one I had been taught about my entire life.

In case you've just furrowed your eyebrows with the "What's Romans 9?" look, it is a passage in which Paul refers back to Jacob and Esau, attributing to God statements such as "JACOB I LOVED, BUT ESAU I HATED." Was I finding a different God? No. It was certainly a difficult passage, but when studied in connection with the Old Testament references (as I did years later in college) it made much more sense to me. Still, it shook me for awhile because instead of looking to the clear, I started focusing for a while on the unclear.

For a long time I disliked the book of Hebrews. I remember the day when our pastor announced that we would be studying through the book of Hebrews on Sunday mornings and that he anticipated that the series would take about a year. It briefly ran through my mind to change churches for a year, but instead I decided to throw myself wholeheartedly into the book.

By the time the year was over and I had invested quite some time in memorization, I loved Hebrews! It wasn't until very recently that I realized that my former distaste probably came from a couple of sticky passages in chapters 6 and 10 that sound at face value as if salvation may be lost. Again, I avoided one of my current New

Testament favorites because I allowed myself to be scared off by the unclear.

Practical Point:* *Watch out for the trap of reading about the Bible instead of reading the Bible

Boy, is this an easy one to fall into. I did this through almost all of college and still fall into this trap occasionally. Realize that reading commentaries and secondary sources provide a great deal of help in Bible study. However, the life-changing power of God comes when we interact with Him through His Word. Commentators, while helpful, simply are not inspired.

The Bible, conversely, describes itself rightly as "God-breathed." Use the commentaries when you are studying in-depth, absolutely, but use them *after* you have done your own study, after you have wrestled with the issues in the text yourself. You will be more informed and be better able to judge the value of the commentators having first worked through the Scriptures yourself.

A couple of other points on commentaries are worth noting. First, make sure that you use more than one commentary so you can compare viewpoints. Second, take care to choose a reputable commentator, one who tells you all the alternate views of interpretation before letting you know why he has chosen his particular view. Other helps in selecting a commentary can be the advice of a pastor or teacher in your church or taking note of the company which has published the book.

***Practical Point:* Major on the majors**

The ungodly major on the minors. The Bible is very clear on this. Paul tells us in II Timothy 2:23, "But refuse foolish and ignorant speculations, knowing that they produce quarrels." The ungodly argue about genealogies and details and weird stuff. They make extra rules, make you jump through extra hoops, and generally get way off track. They make big deals out of unclear passages, building them up into major tenets of the faith while at the same time totally messing up on the major issues, specifically on the person of Jesus Christ.

***Practical Point:* Read history before prophecy**

If you don't understand some of the history of Israel, the Prophets will be very unclear to you. So don't start in Isaiah or Jeremiah or Ezekiel or the Minor Prophets. Before you read the Prophets, get yourself through I and II Samuel and I and II Kings and you'll have a much better base for "getting" the Prophets. Still, they won't be crystal clear right away, so don't fret, just start to get your context.

The Deity of Jesus Throughout the Bible

By following the chain of references listed at the right, you will see how the deity of Jesus Christ spills out of the pages of the Bible. If you've never been a Bible-marker, this would be a good place to start. The references make a giant chain, so the last one on the list brings you back to the first.

Start by turning to Hebrews 1:3–4. In the margin of these verses write the reference of Colossians 2:9–12. Next, turn to Colossians 2:9–12 and mark the reference Colossians 1:15–20 in the margin there. Above each of the references, simply write the word "DEITY." Continue in the same fashion until you arrive back at Hebrews 1:3–4. With this chain, by remembering only one of the references, you'll be able to trace the deity of Jesus Christ through both the Old and New Testaments for yourself, a friend, or a visitor at the front door who you may consider a nuisance, but who is desperately in need of the Savior!

Reference Chain:

- ▼ Hebrews 1:3–4
- ▼ Colossians 2:9–12
- ▼ Colossians 1:15–20
- ▼ John 20:27–29
- ▼ John 17:5
- ▼ Isaiah 42:8
- ▼ Isaiah 7:14
- ▼ Matthew 1:21–23
- ▼ Isaiah 9:6
- ▼ Isaiah 43:10–11
- ▼ Micah 5:2
- ▼ Luke 2:4–7, 10–11
- ▼ Isaiah 44:6
- ▼ Revelation 1:7–8, 17–18
- ▼ John 1:1
- ▼ John 1:14
- ▼ John 8:58–59
- ▼ Exodus 3:14–15
- ▼ John 8:24
- ▼ John 10:30–33
- ▼ Hebrews 1:3–4

For an in-depth look at the deity of Jesus Christ, consider enrolling in a Precept Ministries International Bible study on either the Gospel of John or the book of Hebrews.

THINGS YOU *DO* NEED TO UNDERSTAND:

Before we move on to the next barrier, I need to make a qualification on the one at hand. While you will not understand everything you read in the Bible—and that's okay for the time being—there are a few issues on which you need to be absolutely clear. If you aren't, these are the ones you do need to pursue with diligence sooner than later.

Practical Point: ***You need to be clear on Jesus Christ***

Do you want to be sure that you have the main point of the Bible? Do you want to know that you won't be sucked in by some bizarre heresy? Then get clear on the person and work of Jesus Christ. Don't get into it with the Mormons over "baptism for the dead" or their conception of the levels of heaven. Don't fret over the 144,000 of Revelation and what the Jehovah's Witnesses believe about it. Stick to Jesus and make sure you are clear on Him. This is the point where every heretical teaching will be off. Not *almost* every heresy, *every* heresy. Sure, they'll be off in a lot of other areas, too, but this is the deal-breaker.

Read the Gospels until you understand who Jesus is, the God-man, 100% human, 100% divine. He is not ***a*** god. He did not ***become*** a god. *He is one with God the Father.* He is the I AM of Exodus. Watch how the Old Testament points to Him. Look at the sacrificial system with a view towards the sacrifice of Jesus Christ. See how the prophets point toward Him. Build on the foundation of Jesus, get your Christology right and go from there. Start with the clear and move to the unclear. Get clear on the essentials before you start worrying about issues that people argue over.

For an excellent overview and reference tool, check out the chart on page 89 that shows exactly what the Bible says about the deity of Jesus Christ in both the Old and New Testaments.

Practical Point: ***You need to be clear on the Gospel, the good news of Jesus Christ***

How do you get to heaven? How do you have a right relationship with God? You need to be clear on these. Most people, even those who profess to believe the Bible, think that in some fashion they have to work their way to God. This, however, is clearly not a biblical truth. The biblical truth is that Jesus did the work, not us.

The word "Gospel" means simply "good news." Paul defines that good news in a letter to the church at Corinth, stating in I Corinthians 15:3–8, "For I delivered to you as of first importance what I also received, that Christ died for our sins according to the Scriptures, and that He was buried, and that He was raised on the third day according to the Scriptures, and that He appeared to Cephas [Peter], then to the twelve. After that He appeared to more than five hundred brethren at one time, most of whom remain until now, but some have fallen asleep; then He appeared to James, then to all the apostles; and last of all, as it were to one untimely born, He appeared to me also."

It is here in the first letter to the Corinthians that the components of the good news are very clearly spelled out for us.

- First, CHRIST DIED FOR OUR SINS - Because Jesus Christ was without sin, He could pay the penalty for our sin.
- Second, HE WAS BURIED - He really died; it was not an extended fainting spell.
- Third, HE WAS RAISED ON THE THIRD DAY - When God raised Him from the dead, the power of sin and death was broken. Death cannot hold the Son of God!
- Fourth, HE APPEARED - People actually saw Him. It was not a mere myth or legend. Death had been defeated.

Okay, so He died for my sins, what practically does that mean for me?

What Christ's Death Means for You and Me

Practically, it means that we can have a right relationship with God, and therein be delivered from the power of sin and of death. It means forgiveness and peace in the here and now, and life everlasting in the presence of God.

As it stands right now, if we don't have a relationship with God, we are in deep, deep trouble. We may or may not acknowledge it, but it is truth nonetheless.

The Bible says that we have sinned, we have missed the mark and have fallen short of what God requires, which is absolute perfection. Specifically, it says in Romans 3:23, ". . . for all have sinned and fall short of the glory of God . . ." In our world, this can be a tough concept to accept since we tend to either compare ourselves to others and think we're better at least than they, or to simply conclude that there is no such thing as absolute truth. If truth does not exist, how then can I fall short of a standard that is not real?

The way that this concept makes best sense to me is to think of a swimming race from the coast of San Diego to Hawaii. There is a definite goal: Hawaii. Now, when the gun sounds and we all jump in the water, some would make it further than others would. You might make it further than me, and an Olympic distance swimmer no doubt makes it further than both of us. But make no mistake, none of us would make it without the assistance of a boat, plane, or helicopter. The goal is not attainable, just as the perfect standard of God is not attainable by human beings. Some of us are better than others. Mother Teresa lived an exemplary life. Jesus, Himself,

> ***. . . for all have sinned and fall short of the glory of God . . .***
> ***–Romans 3:23***

speaks incredibly highly of John the Baptist. Neither Mother Teresa nor John the Baptist, however, could match the perfection that God requires. No one comes to God except through Jesus. (John 14:6)

Sorry, but before we can get to the actual Good News of Jesus, the path first gets darker. That is because our sinning and falling short of God's glory comes with a consequence. The Bible calls it a wage. What we earn is death. Romans 6:23 makes this very clear when it states, "For the wages of sin is death . . ."

This is not a good place to be. It is, however, where all humanity is apart from Christ, because none of us can make that swim to Hawaii without help.

Fortunately, God does not leave us here sinking, so to speak, in the middle of the Pacific Ocean of sin. Instead, He reaches out to us in our corrupted condition. Romans 5:6 says, "For while we were still helpless, at the right time Christ died for the ungodly." He brings His one-person helicopter to us in the middle of the ocean, gets into the water and helps us safely aboard the chopper when He became man (incarnate) and died in our place.

For the wages of sin is death . . .
–Romans 6:23

Although Christ died for the ungodly, not all of the ungodly have accepted the gift. So, how do we practically lay hold of this cure that God has affected for our souls?

The Bible tells us in Ephesians 2:8–9 that "For by grace you have been saved through faith; and that not of yourselves, it is the gift of God; not as a result of works, so that no one may boast." The difference between intellectual assent to facts and saving faith is often illustrated by the use of a chair. You can look at a chair and believe in your mind that the chair will support your weight when you sit, but until you actually park your posterior, you have not really trusted it to sustain you.

For while we were still helpless, at the right time Christ died for the ungodly.
–Romans 5:6

Another illustration that works better for me comes from the team-building arena. Several years ago, my husband and I helped lead a group of high schoolers from our church on a leadership retreat. One of the weekend activities was a team-building course where the students would learn to trust one another at a higher level. One of the activities involved putting one student up on a platform with his back to his peers who were standing at ground level. The students on the ground were strategically placed and were instructed to put out their arms to make a human net to catch the student on the platform. The "lucky" one on the platform then had to fall backward off of the platform into the arms of his peers who were located a distance below. Now, each of the kids

> ***For by grace you have been saved through faith; and that not of yourselves, it is the gift of God; not as a result of works, so that no one may boast.***
> ***–Ephesians 2:8–9***

knew that the stunt would work; after all, if it didn't, there would be lawsuits. Still, believing in their heads that their friends would catch them and actually letting go and falling into their arms were two completely different things. The first was intellectual assent, the latter, biblical belief or trust.

I Have to Spend Quality, Alone-time Reading and I Just Don't Have It

Is solitude with God important? Absolutely. Whatever you do, don't read here that alone time with God is not important; it is essential. Followers of Christ know this. We know that we need time to commune with our God. Look at the life of Jesus. He was God incarnate and yet He spent much of His time in solitude communing with His heavenly Father. We don't always do it, but we know that we need to. The problem here, though, is that in the evangelical community we have this term called "quiet time" that we associate with about a fifteen-minute time slot, a devotional (if we're doing really well, an actual Bible), and the absence of other people. In the Old Testament, which was given for our instruction and example, according to the Apostle Paul, we see that the people were instructed to meditate on the Law, the Word of God they had at the time. God instructs Joshua (1:8) saying, "This book of the law shall not depart from your mouth, but you shall meditate on it day and night, so that you may be careful to do according to all that is written in it; for then you will make your way prosperous, and then you will have success." The Hebrew word translated "meditate," means literally, "to mutter." We can't mutter out of our mouths words that are not in our heads and hearts.

If we believe that we have to have perfect "quality" time, many people simply will never make the effort to read.

As I grow in Christ, God draws me into more and more solitude, and on a more regular basis very early in the morning. However, as I began seriously reading the Word earlier in life, it was a very different affair. Back in the day, when my body could still bounce back, my solitude happened almost exclusively at night anywhere from 10 pm to 12 midnight (and later). That doesn't work for my old body anymore, but it once did. God has worked with me in different ways at different times.

This barrier presents a real challenge, especially for people who have become accustomed to filling every moment of every day. If we believe that we have to have perfect "quality" time, many people simply will never make the effort to read. The laundry is never done, the floor is never clean enough, the room is never quiet enough to rest and read. We have guilt if we read in less than perfect conditions. Sure, we can deny it, but other things call our names, other things that are important. Hey, if I had a housekeeper (or was a better one myself) this book would have been finished two years ago.

I'd like to suggest a new paradigm here: "I will give God not only 'quality' time, but 'quantity' time." We use this term when we talk about our kids, so why not God as well? If our kids deserve quantity, how much more so God? And as His children, how much better off are we if we spend not only quality, but also quantity time with Him?

Practical Point: ***Realize that time spent is a priority issue***

We all have 24 hours in a day, with the exception of a couple of Old Testament stories, that is. Thus, to say that you simply do not have the time to read through the Bible when others do comes down to a matter of priority. Sure, some have fewer responsibilities than others, but we all have the choice of our priorities.

Let me illustrate. Let's say I offered you $1,000 cash if you would read just 10 pages of your Bible today. Do you suppose that you could find the time? If I showed up on your doorstep every afternoon at 1:00 p.m. with $1,000 cash for having read just 10 pages of your Bible that day, how many days a week do you surmise that you would miss? Now if, perchance, you made it in the technology sector and got out in time and $1,000 doesn't make the illustration work for you, substitute your own number that would.

Yes, the illustration is extreme. You do, however, see the point, I trust? We can make the time for anything for which we want to make the time. To say that you "just don't have the time" to read your Bible means that you are too busy. Plain and simple. Remember, I said up front that this book was not going to be about political correctness. You choose how you spend your time. Do it wisely.

Practical Point: ***Read in front of your children***

For a big part of the population, children (especially small children) are an easy excuse for not reading the Bible because of their seemingly omnipresent quality. Toddlers are everywhere all of the time. It doesn't matter how early I get up in the morning, my children will wake up 10 minutes later. Some of you understand this totally. Men don't. Those who have never lived with children don't. And those whose children are grown and gone have often experienced some repression! Truth be told, I'm probably a contemplative at heart—put me in a quiet room with my Bible and God and I'm set. But I have children, very talkative ones—and a dog, a very "barky" Dalmatian—and a husband . . . so much for the contemplative lifestyle.

Here's the point: Because of circumstances of life it is easier for some of us to pursue actual "quiet" with God at certain points in time than at others. I prefer to read in the dead quiet, but because of my "life" I've had to learn to read with PBS in the background, with boys running through the house yelling, and with a dog announcing every car coming down our street. Yes, I do read in the quiet sometimes. I need to. In fact, recently, God has been waking me earlier and earlier and making this a new habit. But if I'm looking for real quantity, I have to bloom where I'm planted, so to speak, and in the presence of those who are planted around me.

A funny thing has happened to me lately as I've been reading in front of my kids. They have wanted to join in and help me, something I never would have expected. The Bible I'm currently reading is on my laptop computer. As I read, I'm marking key words and phrases with different colors and symbols. My 9-year old thinks this is just cool beyond belief. Who would have known?

Of course, whatever the 9-year old does, the 4-year old has to do too (her nickname around these parts is "Me Too!"). So I point to the words on the screen that need to be marked and she clicks the mouse and giggles. Don't think I'm going to try and tell you that I read with the same comprehension when I'm being "helped." I usually don't, but I do gain more than if I hadn't been reading at all.

The bigger benefit here, though, is letting my kids see how important the Bible is to me and giving them the opportunity to experience "fun" in Bible study. Sure, they're mainly pointing and clicking at familiar words, but they're associating the Bible with something enjoyable. My son even picked out "joy" as a key word in Philippians. Who'd have thought? As I read, too, I'm able to explain some of what I am reading to them, not out of a devotional or a story book, but directly out of God's Word, which is where I want them to be able to go on their own someday soon.

Of course, I did run into a little trouble the other day when my daughter wanted me to read her the VeggieTales story of *Lyle the Kindly Viking* out of my Bible . . . but I digress.

Practical Point: **Read to your children**

Read to them from your Bible, bringing down the tough words; read to them from children's Bibles, get them *The Visual Bible for Kids** on videotape . . . whatever it takes. Make it a family affair. When they understand how impor-

---

* *The Visual Bible for Kids* is *awesome* and is available from Tommy Nelson™; a division of Thomas Nelson, Inc: Nashville, TN, 2000.

tant the Bible is, they'll probably be more understanding when you want to take some time to read the Bible for yourself. No promises, but give it a try! And always remember your responsibility to teach what you are learning to your children. In fact, if you can't justify the time spent for yourself, do it for them.

Practical Point: Don't be afraid to read in front of others

Now when I say read in front of others, I don't mean sit on the corner of your street like the Pharisees of old and make a big deal of being "religious" and reading your Bible. But if you have time to read and you happen to be around other people, don't feel stupid about reading your Bible.

Now you may protest, "I would never feel embarrassed about reading my Bible." Maybe you're a bigger person than I, but I have to tell you that when I have my Bible out in public sometimes I do feel a little self-conscious. I'm not entirely sure why. Sometimes I think I'm afraid that people will perceive that I think I'm better than they are. Other times, I'm afraid someone will actually ask me about my faith. Sometimes I fear that I'll just look weird. You'll probably have some of those thoughts, too, when you first grab your Bible to read when you're waiting to pick the kids up at school or sitting in the doctor's office or whatever.

My advice, if you'll be "reading out" a great deal, invest in a discreet, cool, smaller Bible that is easy to carry, yet has type that is still readable. Soon you'll pick it up as quickly as you pick up your purse . . . hey, if your purse is big enough, it may fit right in. My husband and dad now have the Bible on their Palm Pilots. I'm not quite into the new millennium yet, but they sure love it, and it might work for you too!

Sub Point: What if reading in public leads to conversations?

This could happen. But guess what! You don't have to have all the answers. Unfortunately, many people never share the faith that they have because they are afraid that they will not be able to answer all of the questions that a potential skeptic could ask them. Realize, though, that a skeptic can always ask more questions than a wise person can answer. That, however, does not make the arguments of the skeptic valid.

If you are a Christian and someone asks you a question about the Bible, the key issue to talk about is the person and work of Jesus Christ. This is the point of the Bible. You don't have to have the answers for the creation/evolution debate or the dating of the age of the earth, the current existence of Noah's ark, the veracity of the story of Jonah, or the like. You need to be clear that God made man, loves man, and sent Jesus, who was fully God and fully man to die on the cross in our place so that we could be forgiven of our sins and be reconciled to a holy God who could not accept us in our sinful state.

The other things are important, but you don't have to have all the answers. You answer for the faith that is in you . . . and that answer has to do with Jesus and what He has done in your life.

Practical Point: ***When you need quiet***

As I write this manuscript it is now summer vacation at my house. We have no morning obligations and I've tried a new plan for quiet. I make sure that I am the first one awake in the house to allow myself some quiet reading time, but then, as soon as the first child wakes up, I let them know that the house is going to be quiet for a certain amount of time, generally ranging from one half hour to an hour, depending on how much I've already been able to read.

It has worked pretty well, and I hope it is teaching my kids to learn silence–something that is in rapid decline in our culture. They are allowed to play quietly, read, go back to sleep, whatever they want as long as they are quiet and allow Mom to have her time with God. If you live alone, you will have a much easier time achieving quiet, but even if you don't, you can work with those you live with to practice the discipline of silence for at least a short time every day. I'm still working on this one, but I'm confident it can be done! Okay, maybe I'm living in a dream world but a girl can hope, can't she?

Practical Point: *Opt for quantity*

It is as though we feel we will dishonor God if we don't have the perfect conditions for reading His Word. We're looking here at the old quality time versus quantity time issue. Let's think about a human illustration here for a minute. Generally speaking, is a small child better off with 10 minutes of quality time with a parent once a day, or by being in the presence of the parent all day through the ups and downs of life?

Please don't misunderstand; I am not saying that you do not need solitude with God. If Jesus did, you and I sure do. Still, we often think that the only time we can read the Bible is when we are alone with God. Wrong answer. We need to think differently!

Think what would happen if you only talked to your spouse or your children or your best friend under perfect conditions. What would happen? Maybe I'm wrong, but I'm thinking the relationship wouldn't end up being that great. So, absolutely find time alone with God, but bring your Bible with you to the doctor's office, to lunch, to the beach. And, no, it is not a sin to read in the bathroom.

Put the Word of God into your heart and mind whenever and wherever you can. Don't forego the quality time alone with Him, but give Him the quantity of time He deserves too. You will be shocked at the difference this can make.

Practical Point: *List your encumbrances*

In Hebrews 12:1–2, the author tells us, "Therefore, since we have so great a cloud of witnesses surrounding us, let us also lay aside every encumbrance and the sin which so easily entangles us, and let us run with endurance the race that is set before us, fixing our eyes on Jesus, the author and perfecter of faith, who for the joy set before Him endured the cross, despising the shame, and has sat down at the right hand of the throne of God."

I recently taught through the book of Hebrews and while I was doing that, God got very serious with me about the encumbrances in my life. Unlike sin, which really is a matter of black and white, encumbrances can be very difficult to identify because they are not necessarily in themselves wrong or bad. Sometimes encumbrances are actually good things that nonetheless keep us from pursuing the best.

Here are some of the things over which I was convicted:

- *Too much stuff* - If you're not what author Sandra Felton, author of *The Messies Manual*,* would term a "Messie," chances are you won't connect with this, but that's okay; bear with me. My house was simply loaded with too much stuff. Sentimental stuff, stuff of memories, but stuff nonetheless. The stuff took too much time to deal with, too much energy. It was always a

* *The Messies Manual* by Sandra Felton, Fleming H. Revell, a Division of Baker Book House Co.: Grand Rapids, Michigan, 1984.

problem lurking in the back of my mind and finally I realized that the stuff was not just a physical issue, but that it had taken on definite spiritual dimensions. It was an encumbrance that needed to be thrown off if I was going to run light for God.

- *Exhaustion entertainment* – Honestly, there are times at the end of the day where I'm too tired to read deeply, to study, or to write. I feel the need to be awake and to be alone, but I am so wiped that I can't do anything productive with the time so I channel surf, stay up later than I should, and wake up even more tired the following morning, perpetuating the cycle.

Practical Point: ***Lay aside the encumbrances***

Sometimes we have to lay old things down to pick newer and better things up. Think with me for a moment of a person weighed down with bags full of garbage. They're wrapped on all his fingers, balanced on the shoulders, and draped over the forearms. The man with his garbage suddenly encounters on the ground a beautiful treasure chest, spilling over with precious jewels. The man cannot carry the garbage and the treasures, so he must choose to lay down the garbage if he wants to pick up the treasure.

We do this all the time. We are so busy with all of our commitments and our stuff; if we are to have the treasure we must set the others aside. We can't do everything, but so often we make the wrong choices. We don't have time for the Word, but we do have time for the newspaper. We can't participate in a Bible study, but we're taking a class at the local college. Or, and I love this one, "I'd love to join that Bible study, but Monday night is my standing hair appointment," or "Jimmy's soccer game," or "my favorite television show," or . . . you fill in the blank.

***Practical Point:* Redeem the time**

In other words, buy back time that is currently being misused or wasted. Always have your reading Bible handy. Always. You never know when you might have a couple of minutes to read.

Sure, it will be a little tough making this into a habit, but women carry purses everywhere, right? You'll get used to it. It's really helpful, I think, to have a Bible with a zipper cover so you can throw a pencil inside and always be ready to mark off your Table of Contents. I've just gotten used to this one. For years, I carried my leather-bound NASB with a pencil stuck in the page where I was reading. Convenient, yes, but not so great on the binding.

***Practical Point:* Get a portable Bible**

Before you pick up that tattered old King James Version and jump in, it's important to remember that you will be spending at least 60 hours with this book on the first pass so it's important to find not only the right translation, but the right style of Bible for your needs.

- *Bible Style* - Bible style? In other words, you need to decide if you are best suited to a small Bible that you can carry around with you everywhere, to a hard back that can take the abuse of, say, small children, or something else. The traditional leather Bible certainly will set you back a couple of dollars, but it will also stand up to a bunch more abuse than a paperback.
- *Translation* - The key here is to find a translation based on the original languages. You might want to stay away from the original King James Version your first time through simply because it is almost as difficult as reading Shakespeare. It was translated for people of another era and it is just plain tough. The New King James, however, is excellent, and compares favorably to my personal favorite, the New American Standard Bible. The New American Standard Bible is very true to the original languages and is, in my opinion, unparalleled as a study Bible. However, it can be a little more difficult to read. For a first time read through the Bible, I would recommend either the New International Version or the New Living Translation. If you're really nervous about reading, go for the New Living Translation. If you're

reading with more of a student's attitude, the New International Version is probably the one to try first.

There are many good translations out there, and throughout your lifetime you'll make it through several of them. Really, you will. As you read, you'll find that you like some better than others, and you may find that you like certain translations for studying and others for your more casual reading. That's normal. I love the New Living Translation for the Old Testament particularly, because it makes the prophets more understandable. However, when it comes to the New Testament, I actually find this more "modern" translation a little tougher to read because I am so familiar with the New American Standard Bible and New International Version renderings of the text. The New Living Translation has a little different cadence to it, which simply slows me down. Read different versions each time through and you'll find on your own which works best for you.

- *Print Size* – Finally, you'll want to make sure that the size of the print is comfortable for you to read. While you may prefer to carry a smaller Bible, this may not be practical if the type size then causes eye strain. If you need larger type, consider purchasing a larger Bible with big type to leave at home for your reading and carry a smaller one with you when you will only be looking at limited references.

***Practical Point:* Try the Bible on audio tape or CD and don't rule out multi-tasking**

I have yet to do this, as I love the written Word, but my husband swears by his New Living Translation on audio tape. As a person with diabetes, he has to exercise everyday, like it or not. So he's started listening to the New Testament on tape as he works out, redeeming the time. I'm thinking that this tape deal (or CD) would probably work in the car, or maybe while I'm cleaning house. Sure, the quality of input may vary, but at least we are picking up something. We will never get the whole deal at once. It is always going to be as Isaiah 28:10 says, ". . .precept upon precept. . . line upon line. . . here a little, and there a little . . . " [KJV]

***Practical Point:* Memorize**

Okay, I know, memorizing isn't exactly going to help you get through the Bible faster, but it is a definite way to start taking the Word with you wherever you go. The more you memorize and meditate on the Word, the more God will use it to transform you and the greater will be your desire for that Word that He has given you. Start with relevant verses, and don't rule out memorizing a chapter or even a book of the Bible. You'll be amazed at what you see when you dig that far and meditate that deeply on God's Word.

I know, I know, you've never been able to memorize, you're too old, or whatever. I'm not buying that excuse. Anyway, consider this one! I personally know people who have memorized entire books of the Bible and it can be done.

Practical Point: ***Photocopy***

Sure, hauling a book around is not always the most convenient thing to do, an average-sized Bible, but who can't fold up a few pieces of paper and throw them in a purse or back pocket? Seriously, run over to your local office supply store and copy the book of Romans. It will probably cost you all of fifty cents and you can have your text with you literally anywhere. Or, get the Bible on CD or find it on a website and print off the books you are reading.

Practical Point: ***Change your default position***

Your computer defaults to certain settings, and if you're honest, you'll admit that you do too! I certainly do!

First, you need to identify your defaults (or should I say "encumbrances"?) and then start to substitute the Bible for your current default positions. For example:

- *Substitute your Bible for other reading material*

  I love to read *Sports Illustrated.* Yes, I'm aware that it's not a typical "chick" magazine, but I love it. Used to come on Thursdays, now it comes on Wednesdays. I only care about the real sports (Cubs baseball, Bulls basketball, and Bears football), but the writing in *SI* is so sublime that if I'm not careful, I'll find myself 12 pages into a 16-page article on synchronized swimming before I even know what's happened. Anything wrong with that? Not really. Could I do better? Of course. Everyone knows that synchronized swimming isn't even a sport! Now, now, everyone's entitled to their opinions on these things, right?

You see while there's nothing wrong with reading *Sports Illustrated,* I need to take care that it doesn't become my "default" read. We all know what a default position is: it's what happens when nothing in particular is happening. For instance, let's say I happen to find myself at home alone at lunchtime (a rarity, I might add). Default for me is to make a salad, pour a diet pop, find something chocolate, sit in the "big chair" and read. If the *SI* is around and I am not being intentional about my choices, I will pick it up. If it's a Wednesday or Thursday, there's usually still something of real interest to me. By the following Tuesday, however, I'm reading about motor sports or figure skating or some other non-sport, just because it's there.

There are times, though, when I'm in the zone, and weeks of magazines will go unread, because I've effectively changed my default position.

- *Substitute your Bible for television*

  Ouch, ouch, ouch!!! Do you have a show that you just have to watch? Do you have two or maybe three? I mean, you'd *just die* if you missed it? If you're not this shallow, then skip to the next section. For the rest of you who are honest, there is hope. Breaking the television habit can be one of the most revolutionary changes that you can make in your walk with Christ . . . but if you're addicted, realize that this is a fight that you won't win on your own, you will only do it through His power. We've all heard it said that everyone has the same 24 hours in a day, but if you're a television addict, realize that you may be pressed for time because you are actually functioning on an adjusted 20-hour day or worse.

  Don't get me wrong here, I'm not trying to say that television is the evil empire and that we should all go back to the non-picture box days. I like a good drama or football game as much as the next guy . . . maybe more, and I've seen in my own life the correlation between my reading habits and television watching. Very simple, actually.

More reading, less television . . . more relaxation and peace of mind. More television, less reading . . . more stress from not getting things done, more chaos, more guilt. One of the great lies of television is that of detachment and relaxation. Let's face it, when you sit down to watch a drama, for example, you can temporarily disengage from your present reality, bringing short-lived relaxation. Sometimes, though, it actually keys you up more if you are drawn into the conflict of the story, because all good stories have conflict! And have you ever noticed that it is exponentially more difficult to turn a television off than to turn it on? I often find that when I sit down to watch one 60-minute show, I'm often dropping a good 2- to 2-1/2 hours before I even realize the time is gone.

So, how to solve this problem? The obvious solution is to just turn the box off. I know, easier said than done. My less-than-spiritual suggestion is to break the habit during reruns. Again, this may not qualify for the spiritual suggestion of the year award, but if you're really addicted, the time when it is easiest to tune out is during reruns. As you tune out the shows you have already seen, you begin to build a habit of not watching that will be easier to maintain as the regular season rolls around. Will this make it easy? No. But it will work. Pray for the endurance and power to break the habit and then schedule other appointments during those times. Go out for coffee with a friend, schedule a racquetball court, go shopping. You may be able to just pick up your Bible during that time, but chances are, you're better off to schedule something out of the house as you begin changing the behavior.

- *Substitute your Bible for video games*

  If you have just rolled your eyes because you cannot figure out at all why someone would ever play a video game, please proceed to the next section. If you're like me, read on. One word: *Tetris.* Two more words: *Space Invaders.* Here's another: *Pikmin.* Laugh if you will, but if you're going to save the world with *Space Invaders,* you'd better clear an hour or 42 minutes if you're as good as me! Of course unless you really watch the clock, the time will just vaporize and you won't even realize how long you've been sitting there. If you're a Windows user, chances are you're also at least slightly addicted to *Free Cell.* Anything wrong with it? No. But it can swallow time if you're not mindful.

- *Substitute your Bible for the Internet*

  My on-line service tells me exactly how many minutes I have spent on-line when I sign off.

More often than not, I'm appalled. What seems like 10 minutes is often closer to an hour. Sure it's flashy and fun, but the Internet drains time (and often morals) with the best of them.

***Practical Point:* Places you can take your Bible, but probably don't**

1. The bathroom
2. The tub
3. The doctor's office or anyplace else you might have to wait
4. A restaurant or cafeteria
5. The beach
6. On vacation
7. Poolside

And yours . . .

8. ______________________________
9. ______________________________
10. ______________________________
11. ______________________________
12. ______________________________
13. ______________________________
14. ______________________________
15. ______________________________

***Practical Point:* If God wakes you up, get up; if God keeps you up, listen to Him, not Oprah**

I find that when I sense a loss of intimacy and quiet with God, when my soul is craving quiet and my life is loud, God has an uncanny knack of waking me a little before five in the morning. When this happens, my natural tendency is to turn over and go back to sleep because I know the rest of my charges are being re-energized, but I find that is always the wrong choice. If God wakes you up, get up and meet with Him.

Similarly, when the house quiets at night and you find yourself overly awake, I promise that you'll find more wisdom in the Word of God than you ever will on the late news or even Oprah rebroadcasts (although her friend Dr. Phil has a lot of good things to say)!

***Practical Point:* Go on a personal retreat**

Several years ago, on a retreat for adult leaders of our church's high school ministry, our youth pastor had an interesting afternoon planned for all of his volunteer staff. He sent us out for two hours. Each person took only himself and his Bible and spent the next two hours alone with God out in the field, in the woods, wherever, just so long as they had solitude. Leaving the meeting area, the faces told the story on many individuals, "Two hours? What on earth am I going to do for two hours alone with just my Bible?"

At the end of the weekend, however, person after person shared how those very two hours were unexpectedly, by far, the highlight of the weekend. Now, I know what you're thinking; this must not have been a very fun group. Quite the contrary. We had all worked together for years and had great fun playing together on these leadership retreats, and yet when it came down to it, the two hours of solitude allowed God to break into lives in very significant ways.

Taking a step further, you may wish to go away to a retreat center or a local house of prayer for an overnight or a weekend. In the Chicago area where I live, there is a small house of prayer located in one of the southwestern suburbs that is run by a group of Catholic Sisters. I've never experienced quiet on the scale that I do there. The accommodations are very homey. Each of the six rooms has a single bed, a reading chair and lamp, a small desk, and a sink. The six rooms share two full and immaculately clean bathrooms. For meals, you can choose to bring food back to your room or share meals with the sisters. It is simply a wonderful place to be alone with God. The Sisters welcome Catholics and Protestants alike, and focus on what we have in common which is so much greater than the areas in which we differ.

Practical Point: ***Learn quiet***

You may just have a problem of avoiding quiet. Think about how our society works today; we avoid quiet at all costs. We have televisions not only in the living room or the family room, but often in bedrooms too. We have radios and CD players in our houses and our cars. We even carry them on our bodies. Background music is everywhere. Where do you think the term "elevator" music came from? Why on earth do we need music for a trip in an elevator?

Think about your own habits for a minute. What is the first thing you do when encountered with quiet? Do you reach for the remote, for the phone, for the radio? Most of us do. It's the culture in which we have been raised and it flies in the face of learning solitude.

Practical Point: **Learn to block noise**

You can learn to block noise. It is not easy, but it can be done. Right now, I'm writing with the *Wild Thornberrys* in the background. Sorry, if that's not good enough for you, but that's my life! When I was in high school, my husband, okay, he was my boyfriend at the time, was a sound engineer for a Christian rock band. I spent the better part of one summer sitting in a sound studio with rock and roll blaring . . . and I mean blaring . . . reading *Gone with the Wind.* Sure, it was a little tough at first, but I learned to focus on the text and ignore the background sound, loud as it was.

My third grade son, however, cannot do his math homework with his sister so much as whispering in the background. Somehow I think it's just a hang-up with not wanting to do the homework. Just a guess.

Practical Point: ***Ice cream and the Chicago Cubs***

I am a die-hard Cub fan. (If you don't live near Chicago, you can't fully understand.) Anyway, a treat in our house during the middle of the summer is to stay up late when the Cubbies are playing on the west coast and eat ice cream while we ignore bedtimes and watch baseball. My 4-year-old daughter was turning into a huge baseball fan over the summer. She absolutely loved the Cubs . . . I thought. But as we made our way into autumn and the Cubs were no longer playing, I came to realize that it was not so much my beloved Cubbies, but her beloved ice cream. We had a Pavlovian response going on. Ice Cream . . . Baseball . . . Ice Cream . . . Baseball. Stick with me here.

If you really hate to read, why not set up a Pavlovian response. Make your reading time a real treat. Sit in your favorite chair with your favorite treat if that's what it takes to get yourself going. Who's to say you can't set up a system of Bible . . . Ice cream . . . Bible . . . Ice cream. Associate your reading with something really enjoyable if reading itself is not enjoyable to you. Shallow? Probably, but it could just work! Hey, it wouldn't surprise me that my daughter may just be the first female shortstop in the major leagues due to the ice cream connection!

I Have to Stick to a Strict Schedule if I'm Going to Make It

There is, in my estimation, nothing much more depressing than having a perfect schedule and falling behind. I don't know about you, but I'm great at making complex and meticulous lists and terrible about keeping them. The planning's fun, but the doing is a drag, which probably accounts for the reason I can't follow other people's Bible reading schedules. Not only do you have to "do it," you don't even have the fun of planning it out! Miss a day, and you're forever trying to catch up. The reading piles up like unattended laundry in a house full of dirty young boys. Maybe you are a schedule-keeper. Maybe you can read exactly what you're told to read every day for 365 days. I'm guessing you're not, however, since you're reading this book! If you are a schedule keeper, though, there are plenty of good ones out there to follow. You're now dismissed. Find a schedule and enjoy a Book much more edifying than this one!

For those of you who are left, I have some great news! You don't need a schedule to read through the Bible! In their defense, schedules do help some people. People like me, however, they simply frustrate.

This barrier sets you up for failure and guilt, and moves the reading of God's Word into the academic realm instead of the relationship realm. Instead of thinking, "I have to read X number of chapters a day," try thinking, "I have the privilege of spending one-on-one time with the God of the universe every day." Here are some other suggestions to help you break this barrier.

***Practical Point:* Remember that it's a relationship**

We've talked about this a little already, but the importance bears repeating. How do your relationships hold up when you ignore them? Sure, there are some relationships that you can put on hold occasionally that don't suffer, but just think what life would be like if you went through the day ignoring, for example, your spouse, your son or your daughter. Even the dog gets bent if she doesn't get her fair share of time. Why should we think that we can maintain a right relationship with our God if we do not invest time with Him? In fact, a relationship with God should be the primary relationship of our lives, since it is the one that will provide the glue for all of the other relationships. I have the power to love my husband and children in a much greater fashion when God is my first love. Second place to God is much higher than first place without Him.

***Practical Point:* Don't let yourself get too academic**

As I mentioned, one of the main reasons I dislike Bible reading schedules is that they move the reading into the academic realm. Now, you need to understand here that I love the academic realm. I am a student at heart, always have been. We encounter problems, though, when we get so academic with the Bible that we divorce it from application. Knowledge and study without prayer and application puffs up. So study and learn but never without praying and applying what you learn to your life or you run the risk of becoming puffed up with dead doctrine.

***Practical Point:* Make "appointments" with God and accept if He takes the initiative**

There are times in my life when pursuing time with God becomes incredibly difficult. When we are too busy, we need to make "appointments" with God. Just as you would set a time on the calendar for a dear friend, mark out a time when you can meet with God uninterrupted. Put it on the calendar and don't schedule over it. At times of crisis, when you feel your soul starving for God, be aware when He takes the initiative. I've had times of intense busyness when I've been crying out to God for time to meet with Him; times when I've felt the intense need to sit quietly in His presence, but have had screaming toddlers and other responsibilities from which I simply could not divest myself.

I've found that at times like these, when I've been crying out to God for time to spend with Him, that I am awakened in the middle of the night or very early in the morning–I mean really awake (which I never am naturally–at least not in the past nine years!). The first time this happened, I went for about three nights running, waking up and just being annoyed before I finally suspected that God was answering my prayer for time alone with Him. Although I had been thinking more along the lines of my husband taking the kids out for the day, God, apparently, had another way of providing that quiet time that I needed. I just didn't quite "get it" at first.

Practical Point: ***Even better, make general habits***

Before I say anything else, I need to say this: I need work here. I usually do read every day, but timing for me over the years has varied like the snowflakes. I tell myself that this is because of my stage in life and that it will get better when my kids get older, and honestly, I think it will. In fact, this is an area in which God has been working lately. The fact that my time of day varies sets me up for potential problems, the biggest of which is that God can simply be pushed out by fatigue if I haven't read my Bible before the end of the day. Being a night owl, I often do read late when the house quiets down, but sometimes I have simply had it all sucked out of me by then.

A good friend and mentor of mine who has a set "time of day" explains that she would no sooner leave the house in the morning without having spent time with God than she would leave the house without taking a shower, brushing her teeth, or combing her hair. That is the direction I have sensed God moving me, towards more of an early to bed, early to rise mentality.

Maybe this concept will connect with you, especially if you're the "I-can't-leave-the-house-without-my-makeup" type. Personally, if I'm clean and I have a baseball cap, I'll go just about anywhere if push comes to shove, which obviously demonstrates my issues with routine. Now I've probably said too much, so let's move on . . .

Practical Point: ***Set a final goal and give yourself a reward***

Rewards. Does this sound really unspiritual to you? Probably so. But let's face it, sometimes a little incentive can make you move. Rewards work for kids, right? Why? Because they're fun! They give you the incentive to put things in gear. Several years ago after my second baby, I had held on to several extra pounds, and I was not alone. Three of my friends were also struggling to lose post-baby weight. Instead of suffering alone, we set up a little accountability group and contest. First one to take off ten pounds won a pot of about $50. Now it wasn't that much money, but just the game of it, the potential reward, kept a bunch of chocolate out of my mouth. It kept me drinking my water and exercising four days a week.

Now, I'm encouraging rewards simply because they work. Did you realize, though, that the concept is entirely biblical? Not like we work to get to heaven or that God gives us every temporal desire. That, you'll find out quickly, isn't the biblical way, but throughout both the Older and Newer Testaments we find God talking about rewards.

As early as Genesis 15:1b we see God telling Abram, "Do not be afraid, Abram. I am your shield, your very great reward." [NIV] Later, in one of the most famous of biblical chapters, the so-called faith chapter in Hebrews, we read that the one who comes to God must believe "that He is and that He is a rewarder of those who seek Him." We see, too, in Hebrews 11 that Moses followed God and gave up the passing pleasures of Egypt, because he was looking to the reward. God is a rewarder. You'll see this when you read.

So set a reward for finishing, and make it worth attaining. How about a leisurely weekend away or maybe a shopping excursion for something special. Be sure to make the treat something that you want and don't let yourself have it until you do the job.

***Practical Point:* Set checkpoints with mini rewards**

The only thing that works better than big rewards are little rewards along the way!

So why not give yourself some little treats when you make progress in your Bible reading? It doesn't need to be anything big . . . just enough to keep you going. Maybe you'll treat yourself to dinner out with a friend or maybe you'll treat yourself to a new blouse or an espresso. Who knows, maybe it will even be that great Greek-based, hard-back commentary on Hebrews at your local seminary bookstore that you couldn't break down and spend the $39.95 on! Okay, or maybe not . . .whatever works for you. But make it fun! Now, will you have to treat yourself for the rest of your life to keep you reading the Bible? Hopefully not. This is just one of those ways to train yourself and make it fun to get into the habit of the Bible.

Make sure that you have treats set up for finishing Leviticus, Numbers, each one of the big prophets (Isaiah, Jeremiah, Ezekiel), Acts, and Revelation.

***Practical Point:* Don't set a chapter per day quota**

Whatever you do, don't set a chapter per day quota. Okay, I know that most of you will pull out a calculator to do the math, so let me save you the time. To make it through the Bible in a year, you'll need to average about 3 chapters a day. But please, please, please don't read 3 chapters a day or you'll miss the flow and turn a relationship into an assignment. Read logical portions. Stop at the end of an epistle, read through the conclusion of a story, don't just stop because you've "done your time." I think back here to when my son was in the second grade. Each day he had to read for 30 minutes. At the outset, it didn't matter if he was mid-sentence when the timer went off, HE WAS FINISHED. Reading was a chore and all he wanted was to be done! One day, however, he asked if he could read a joke book for his reading time. I told him that he could read the back of a ketchup bottle if he wanted to, he just had to read! This revolutionized his reading time. Since then, he has learned to enjoy reading (well, some of the time. . . he's a boy!).

Practical Point: ***Read in "chunks"***

Slow and steady may win the race, but reading a couple of minutes a day is not how we read most books. So why should we read the Bible any differently? One of the best ways to actually "connect" with what you are reading is to set aside a couple of hours and just go at it. Think about how hard it is to get into a novel when you only let yourself read one page. Same thing with the Bible; so much of it is narrative that just doesn't lend itself to ten-minute reads. You'll be amazed at what God will do if you just set aside two hours of time to spend alone with Him and His Word.

This is an especially good idea if you're just starting out with a serious reading program. Take the time to immerse yourself in the Word and to rid yourself of the fear that you can't do it. When you get right down to it, isn't that half the problem, the fear that you'll start and fail?

Here are some typical books I like to read when I'm "chunk" reading:

- Historical books: Genesis (often termed "Law," but is historical in nature); Joshua and Judges; I and II Samuel; I and II Kings; Ezra and Nehemiah.
- Prophetic books: Daniel and Revelation
- Any of the Gospels
- The book of Acts

Reading in chunks also helps us to stop looking at the clock. What is it about clocks that is so fascinating anyway?

***Practical Point:* Read in logical progressions**

As you read, you will tend to find that certain books lead to other books. When you find certain books linking to others, follow the chain. You may not be able to figure these out the first time you read through, but the more you read, the more you will discover strands of thought that will lead you from one book to another. The first time I read through the Bible, for instance, I started in I Samuel; this led to II Samuel and then to the Kings. Any beginning reader would be able to figure this out just by reading. At the end of the Kings, we see the people going into captivity. With a little biblical history in my back pocket, I realized that the books of Daniel, Jeremiah, and Lamentations took place during this time of captivity, so I moved on to those books in my reading.

The New Testament books of Luke and Acts were written by the same author, Luke, the physician. The Gospel of Luke tells the story of Jesus from Luke's point of view, and Acts is a continuation of the story, telling of Jesus' ascension to heaven and the story of the early church. In the New Testament you can also follow the train of thought of a given author in reading the writings of the Apostle John or of Paul, for instance. John penned the Gospel bearing his name, as well as I, II, and III John. He also wrote the prophetic book of Revelation, while Paul wrote most of the New Testament letters (sometimes called epistles), including Romans, I and II Corinthians, Galatians, Ephesians, Philippians, Colossians, I and II Thessalonians, I and II Timothy, Titus, and Philemon.

Practical Point: ***Accept grace***

As I mentioned earlier, I'm a recovering perfectionist. I hate messing up. I can't stand doing something wrong. It pains me to my bones to fall short of a goal that I've set, and as a perfectionist, the goals that I set are always way too high. In other words, I have a very strong inborn tendency to beat myself up when I don't perform up to my own expectations. Now, I may outperform others, but that for me is not enough if I know I have not done my best. I can accept imperfection in others (well, usually), but learning to accept it in myself has been tough, and yet I am so fraught with imperfections. So when you mess up and go for a week without reading, realize that you are human, ask God's forgiveness and help, and get back on the horse. Don't dwell on the mistakes and failures, look forward and bask in the love that God lavishes on you and move toward Him.

Our tendency when we aren't performing as we should is to shrink back, to stop trying, and to drift, at least that is my tendency. This is exactly what our adversary wants . . . for us to float through life, not making any waves at all. Instead, when we aren't on the top of our game, we need to draw near to God, knowing that He loves us, warts and all. We need to accept that we are saved by grace and that we also grow by grace (Galatians 3:3), and that we will never be good enough on our own. It is all God.

Practical Point: **Relax**

Enjoy the Word. Be diligent, yes. But don't be uptight. Don't set the clock, don't get the guilts and try to make it up if you miss a day. Find a comfortable spot to sit, put your feet up, and learn to enjoy spending time with your God. View your time in His Word as a time of rest and restoration. If reading through in a year is too fast for you, then find out what is comfortable and go for it.

***Practical Point:* Think of reading as a "get to do" instead of a "got to do"**

At my children's school, they are extremely security cautious and strictly limit the number of parents at each class party. In fact, with only four moms (or dads) per party, the only way a person has any chance of attending all parties is by being in charge—being the Big Kahuna (or Head Room Mom as they prefer to call it). This past year was my first as the Big Kahuna, and not just a little stressful since I am still learning what works and doesn't work with grade school children.

On one particularly busy day of the week of the politically correct "Holiday Party," all of the last minute "stuff" seemed like such a burden. I was on my way to a cranky old day when I realized that "I don't *have to* do this, I *get to* do this." At that moment my paradigm shifted dramatically.

What an opportunity I had. How many others would have liked to do what I was getting to do but couldn't because of work commitments and other encumbrances? How fortunate I was to have this fun opportunity with my son and his classmates! How fortunate are you to have a Bible and to be able to meet with God, and without fear of persecution!

***Practical Point:* Watch out for the trap of always "preparing" to start, always thinking about it and never doing it**

I like to *plan* to do things, but sometimes the actual *doing* of them can get a little tough. Right now, you are preparing to start, because you're reading this book. Hopefully this will be of assistance to you, but don't get stuck here. Don't spend your Bible-reading time making a schedule to follow or reading commentaries about the Bible. Don't waste your time reading footnotes or general inspirational literature. Read the Bible. Jump in and go for it. Pray and move forward. As mentioned before, commentaries are great, inspirational and devotional books can be a help, but they need to be *in addition* to the Bible, not *in place* of it. They are not God-breathed. The Bible is!

Practical Point: ***Track yourself in writing***

Have you ever been on a diet? Up until a few years ago, I never had been. I was always a pretty skinny, athletic kid, but then I grew up and had children. Enough said. Anyway, when it was finally time to drop a few pounds, I found that writing down what was going into my mouth was the best way to keep the right things in and the wrong things out.

If I don't journal when I diet, I don't lose weight. I have no way of benchmarking and assessing progress. It is the same in reading your Bible, particularly when you're not reading sequentially. No matter how well you comprehend what you read, you're going to lose track of which of the 66 books you have and have not read if you're not writing it down. The easiest way to do this is to use your Table of Contents.

***Practical Point:* Use your Table of Contents**

We discussed this along with Barrier #1, but just in case you're skimming, I want to make sure that you don't miss this point. A pencil and your Table of Contents are by far the simplest and, I think, best way to keep track of your reading. Don't worry about an elaborate schedule that you need to keep, boxes you need to check off, or a matrix the size of your wall to track yourself. Simply jot down your start date by your Table of Contents, pencil in the goal for completion (give yourself a year the first time through), and make sure that you read in the same Bible until you're done.

This may sound silly, but you want to be able to read and record right away without any hassles. The lower the hassle factor, the higher the chance that you'll follow through. When I record books that I've read, I always do it in pencil so that I can erase my marks and use the same Bible for another read-through. Sometimes I simply mark the books read with a simple check mark; other times through, I've dated the books by the month finished. The point here is that you have a simple, accessible way to track your progress so that you always know where you are.

Occasionally, I read more than one book concurrently as I rarely have what it takes to read straight through Isaiah, Ezekiel, or the Psalms. In cases where I am reading more than one book, I usually make a distinct mark next to the books I am currently reading, using just a dot to remind myself that I have begun a particular book. I then either keep a bookmark at the point I left off or simply mark my end point with a pencil.

Practical Point: ***Experiment***

As you're learning to read your Bible, experiment a bit. Try reading at different times of the day. Try different parts of the house. Read while you eat. Read without eating. Read in the chair, read in bed, read at the kitchen table. Read on your computer, read out of your regular Bible. Memorize. I can give you pointers, other people can give you tips, but in the end, you have to find what works for you and you won't figure out what's best if you haven't tried some different approaches.

Practical Point: ***Ask around for advice***

Don't be shy in asking others for advice. Chances are you know people who are serious students of God's Word. Ask what works for them and what doesn't. Allow yourself to be mentored or discipled by such people in your life. This isn't a sign of weakness . . . it's a sign of smarts. Really. Sure, as tough Westerners, we think we can figure everything out by ourselves. You know there are tons of things we *can* figure out on our own, but why on earth should we stumble forward when we can stand on the shoulders of others and learn from their successes and failures?

Practical Point: ***Do what works for you***

Go with what works for you. My husband can read at Caribou Coffee. The ambient noise there would drive me nuts. I, however, can read with the noise of kids in the background. Some people need the early morning, some people need the late night. Really what works for people varies. Figure out what works best for you and do it. This does not include the option of saying, "Nothing works for me." Some things will work better for you than others. Stick with it until you find what works the best for you and keep going.

Practical Point: ***Keep moving and don't give up***

Don't underestimate the importance of momentum. And whatever you do, don't punt. If you realize that you can't make it through in a year, so what? Reassess your goals and keep moving. There's nothing magical about reading through the Bible in a year, but it is important to keep going and keep making progress.

When you're sitting still it's hard to get moving. Physics, my Dad tells me, teaches us that a body in motion tends to stay in motion. The same thing is true here. Once you get moving, it's much easier to stay moving than to start and stop and start again. Even if you have to move slowly, keep moving.

I Can't Do It

There are a few words that draw a response from me every time they are uttered in my house. One of the biggies is the phrase "I can't." "But Mom, I can't . . ." will always bring me out of my shell. Whenever one of my kids spouts up with an "I can't" statement, I chime in with, "Don't you mean, you have not yet been able to." Sure, my son thinks it's an issue of semantics (even though he doesn't yet know what that word means), and you may too, but that doesn't change the fact that there is a world of difference between saying "I CANNOT" do something, and "I have yet to do it." The first takes the pessimistic and easy way out. Failure accepted right from the beginning somehow hurts less since there is nothing invested.

The truth here, however, is that if you are reading this book, if you can read the newspaper, or a magazine, you can read the Bible. Before the advent of more modern translations, understanding the phraseology was sometimes an issue, but with newer translations the simple truth is, if you can read, you can read the Bible. Not only that, even if you're a terrible reader, if you can simply understand the spoken word, you can listen to the entire Bible on audiotape or CD. There is no excuse for not ingesting the Word of God.

Practical Point: *Pray!*

I don't mean to be simplistic here, but praying and reading the Bible go together in more ways than just understanding what you're reading. One of the biggest keys I found in having the desire for God's Word and the stamina to keep on moving is consistently praying for that desire. Do you think that it is God's will that His children desire His Word? Of course it is! And what does He promise about prayers that are asked in accordance with His will? He says that He will hear them and answer them. (I John 5:14–15)

God has a plan. When we align ourselves with that plan and pray in accordance with it, we will see results. It is like swimming downstream. I could pray tomorrow that God would drop a million bucks in small bills on my front porch. Does He have the power to do it? Sure. Will He? I can't imagine that He would, as this would not align with His purpose. However, if we pray for a desire for His Word, this does align with His Word and purpose in our lives. As followers of Christ, God's purpose is to transform us into the likeness of His Son and His Word plays a huge part in this transformation.

If your desire for the Word has been quenched, pray. If necessary, pray and fast for that desire which you know is of God. Continue to pray that God would put a burning desire in your heart for His Word and His ways.

Practical Point: *Get accountable*

There's nothing that will give you a better initial kick in the pants to get going and to keep going than having to answer to another human being about what you have or have not been reading. This person needs to be someone who's close enough so that you can be honest when you don't measure up, but distant or respected enough that you won't fall into the "lazy" routine. What, you ask, is the lazy routine? It goes something like this:

Week 1:

Pam: Boy, I'm so excited about reading through the Bible this year! This is great isn't it?

Friend: Yeah, I'm just on fire! I read I Samuel this week and next week I'm going to read the Gospel of John!

Pam: Wow! That's great! This week I read Romans, and next week I'm going to get through Genesis, and maybe start Exodus if I'm really on a roll!

Friend: Great! I'll see you next week.

Week 2:

Pam: So, how'd this week go for you? It was a little tough on me.

Friend: It went okay, but not as well as I'd been hoping. Boy, I was just so tired, and the kids were just awful.

Pam: Yeah? Mine too.

Friend: So, it ends up I was going to read all of John, but I ended up only getting through the first three chapters.

Pam: Sounds like my week. I was reading in Genesis and only got up to Cain and Abel.

Friend: Oh well, it was a hard week. Some weeks are like that, right?

Pam: Oh absolutely. I had meetings two nights this week. My son had basketball practice. Then we had games all weekend. Oh, by the way, I can't meet next week. I'm in this drama at church.

Friend: That's all right. We'll just meet the following week. I'll keep going in John and you'll keep working in Genesis, right?

Pam: You got it. See you in two weeks.

Week 3:

Pam: Things just seem to get busier and busier.

Friend: Here I thought it was just me. I have to be

honest. I haven't read since the last time we met. I feel really bad about it, but there's just so much going on.

Pam: I have to tell you, you've just made me feel a lot better about myself! I haven't had a chance to read either. Life has just been so crazy.

Friend: You want to go for some coffee?

Pam: Yeah, sure, but I need to be home by 9:00. There's a new episode of my favorite show on tonight; I never miss it.

Friend: Oh that's right, I've gotta get home too!

You get the point. The Bible says in Proverbs 27:17, "Iron sharpens iron, So one man sharpens another." But, you know as well as I that there are far more cardboard friends out there than iron ones. In the realm of accountability it is critical to not only find, but to be, an iron friend.

***Practical Point:* Accept the fact that reading the Bible is NOT rocket science**

God put the Bible in the language of the common man. The New Testament was not written in high style classical Greek, but in Koine Greek, the common Greek language of the day. Jewish boys learned the Torah, the first five books of the Old Testament. The Bible was never intended to be a coffee table book that just sits there looking good or a shelf book that you have "just because every house needs one."

The simple fact is "The Bible is NOT Rocket Science!" We like to believe it is, because in some way we feel that excuses us from the responsibility to live by its statutes. If we can't understand, we reason, how could God ever hold us to what is in it? But it is not rocket science, it is within our grasp. We need desperately to accept that fact and to bring that word to others.

Practical Point: ***Accept your weaknesses***

You are human. You are fallen. That's okay. Jesus loves fallen humans, so much that He died for the whole lot of us. If you're thinking that you probably can't pull this one off by yourself, honestly, you're probably right. Stuart Smalley of *Saturday Night Live* fame might have you tell yourself, "I'm good enough, I'm smart enough, and doggone it, people like me," but I sure won't. Because you're not good enough without God. With Him, absolutely; without Him, you will more than likely fail.

The beauty here is that the Bible tells us that God's power is perfected in our weakness (II Corinthians 12:9). And that is where we need to focus, on the power that is at work within us, not on our own frailties!

Practical Point: ***When you run into the Prophets, realize they speak the Words of God***

Here is a possible exception to the pencil rule we discussed earlier. If you think you can't read the Major Prophets, get a highlighter and start highlighting the words of God in the text. When you realize that these books are filled with God's specific words, it puts a different spin on it and makes it a lot easier to read . . . at least it did for me.

***Practical Point:* Realize who you are in Christ and what power is really at your disposal**

Have you ever read the New Testament book of Ephesians?

Get this from the New American Standard:

> *"I pray that the eyes of your heart may be enlightened, so that you will know what is the hope of His calling, what are the riches of the glory of His inheritance in the saints, and what is the surpassing greatness of His power toward us who believe. These are in accordance with the working of the strength of His might which He brought about in Christ, when He raised Him from the dead and seated Him at His right hand in the heavenly places, far above all rule and authority and power and dominion, and every name that is named, not only in this age but also in the one to come. And He put all things in subjection under His feet, and gave Him as head over all things to the church, which is His body, the fullness of Him who fills all in all."*
>
> *–Ephesians 1:18–23*

I love this one so much that we're going to look at it in the New Living Translation as well. If this doesn't knock you between the eyes, I don't know what will!

> *"I pray that your hearts will be flooded with light so that you can understand the wonderful future he has promised to those he called. I want you to realize what a rich and glorious inheritance he has given to his people.*
>
> *"I pray that you will begin to understand the incredible greatness of his power for us who believe him. This is the same mighty power that raised Christ from the dead and seated him in the place of honor at God's right hand in the heavenly realms. Now he is far above any ruler or authority or power or leader or anything else in this world or in the world to come. And God has put all things under the authority of Christ, and he gave him this authority for the benefit of the church. And the church is his body; it is filled by Christ, who fills everything everywhere with his presence."*
>
> *–Ephesians 1:18–23, (NLT)*

Whoopee!!!

Did you notice *everything* that we have in Christ Jesus?!

IN CHRIST JESUS:

- God has blessed us in the heavenly realms with every spiritual blessing in Christ.
- He chose us in Him before the creation of the world to be holy and blameless in His sight.
- He gives us His glorious grace in Christ.
- In Christ, we have redemption through His blood, the forgiveness of sins, in accordance with the riches of God's grace that He lavished on us with all wisdom and understanding.
- In Christ, we were chosen.
- In Christ we hope.
- We were included in Christ when we heard the Word of truth.
- Having believed, we were marked in Christ with a seal, the promised Holy Spirit, who is a deposit guaranteeing our inheritance.
- We have His incomparably great power for us who believe. That power is like the working of His mighty strength, which He exerted in Christ when He raised Him from the dead and seated Him at His right hand in the heavenly realms, far above all rule and authority and power and dominion, and every title that can be given, not only in the present age but also in the one to come.
- God raised us up with Christ and seated us with Him in the heavenly realms in Christ Jesus, in

order that in the coming ages he might show the incomparable riches of His grace, expressed in His kindness to us in Christ Jesus.

- We are God's workmanship, created in Christ Jesus to do good works, which God prepared in advance for us to do.
- In Christ we who were far away have been brought near through the blood of Christ.
- In Christ we are being built together . . .
- We are sharers together in the promise in Christ Jesus.
- God's eternal purpose was accomplished in Christ Jesus.
- In Christ and through faith in Him we may approach God with freedom and confidence.
- Truth is in Christ Jesus.
- In Christ, God forgave us.

What kind of power does the follower of Christ have according to Ephesians? The same mighty power that raised Christ from the dead! That's power! And if you belong to Christ, that is the power that He uses in your life. It doesn't matter how weak you think you are . . . that kind of power is enough for anybody!

Practical Point: ***Explore the spiritual disciplines***

The spiritual disciplines have been largely lost by today's Evangelical culture. Nonetheless, they are invaluable as aides to spiritual growth and formation. Realize that these are not ends in themselves, but merely tools to use along the spiritual journey.

The disciplines are generally grouped differently by different authors, for example,

Richard Foster, *Celebration of Discipline,** looks at them as Inward, Outward, and Corporate:

- **Inward**: Meditation, Prayer, Fasting, and Study
- **Outward**: Simplicity, Solitude, Submission and Service
- **Corporate**: Confession, Worship, Guidance, and Celebration

Dallas Willard, *The Spirit of the Disciplines,*† looks at them as Disciplines of Abstinence and Engagement:

- **Disciplines of Abstinence**: Solitude, Silence, Fasting, Frugality, Chastity, Secrecy, and Sacrifice
- **Disciplines of Engagement**: Study, Worship, Celebration, Service, Prayer, Fellowship, Confession, and Submission

For a full discussion on the disciplines, you'll need to check out either Foster or Willard as that lies well beyond the scope of this book. However, let me quickly note that

---

* *Celebration of Discipline,* by Richard J. Foster, San Francisco, California: Harper & Row Publishers, 1978.

† *The Spirit of the Disciplines,* by Dallas Willard, San Francisco, California: HarperSanfrancisco, 1988.

solitude with God will change your life. When you try fasting, you'll realize that it is not just for an age gone by. And simple living with less stuff translates into more time. Don't believe it? Try it and see for yourself.

Foster and Willard are both great reading, but make it through your Bible first!

Practical Point: Start a group

While the accountability of another individual works best for some people, others may find the support and encouragement they need in a group. Consider forming a group that will read through the Bible together over the course of a year or two. When I say "read together" I'm not talking about reading the same material at the same pace, but rather having a group that meets once a month or so to share with one another where each person has been reading and how things are going. Hopefully you'll have at least one or two strong people in the group who can encourage and exhort the weaker members to continue on and finish.

Another upside to a group is that when you begin sharing with each other where you are reading and how it is going, you will be alerted to difficult areas, as well as really good books, through the experience of others in the group. When you see another of flesh and blood actually succeed and make it through Leviticus or Isaiah, then you'll gain that extra measure of encouragement to know that you can make it, too!

***Practical Point:* Enlist someone to pray for you in your mission**

Sure, you'll feel stupid if you ask someone to pray for you and then you fail. But guess what?! The odds that you will fail go down dramatically if you seek out a prayer warrior to help you on your mission. I'm not talking here about just asking your best friend to pray for you, not unless that person is a true prayer warrior.

Be watchful of the people in your church; find out who has the gift of intercession. Ask God to lead you to the right person or people to pray for you, and ask them to help pray you through your mission. When you run into tough times, call them with specific prayer requests. When you have success let them rejoice with you.

***Practical Point:* Talk about what you read**

Okay. This is going to seem a little weird at first, especially if you hang out with people who are biblically illiterate. However, talking with someone about what you are reading helps you not only to process what you are taking in, but it helps to connect the Bible to your daily life. When you verbalize what you read, you begin to interact with it on another level, because to be able to talk about something you've read means you need to read with a degree of comprehension. You can't just rip through five pages, make a check mark in a box, and be on your way. To talk about something intelligently, you need to be a careful reader. You need to be interacting with the text, looking for the point, trying to understand. All of a sudden, relevance increases, if from nothing more than the fact that it has become a center of discussion in your real-life conversations.

Additionally, when something comes out of your own mouth, you will tend to have more "buy in" to the application. Several years ago, my husband and I participated in a parenting class. One of the points that was stressed in helping children to obey was to call for a verbal response. For instance, when I ask my son to come to the dinner table, it is his job to answer with an affirmative, "Yes, Mom." Similarly, if I am giving instructions to a smaller member of the family, I will ask the child to repeat back to me what they are going to do. In that repeating back of the information, they not only remind themselves of the instructions, but by verbalizing it with their little mouths, they have a higher degree of "buy in." Does it always work? No. Does anything? Seriously, though, it does help.

Practical Point: ***Take someone else along for the ride***

Once you get on a roll and start making progress in your Bible reading, take someone else along for the ride. Now, you may already have a partner or group that you're reading with. That's fine. Find others to join you on the way. As you begin to see success in your reading, share that excitement with others and encourage them. There will doubtless come a time in your spiritual life when you'll need someone to come along and give you encouragement. So while you're rolling, don't be selfish, reach out and lovingly spur others on and encourage them in their walks!

Practical Point: ***Anticipate and prepare for opposition***

Satan doesn't want you reading the Bible. I don't know how to say it more simply. Cut off from the Word of God, you are spiritually impotent. Do nothing and you are of no real concern to the adversary; you're actually playing on his team. But get yourself into the Word of God and you become an armed soldier.

Does this mean we should let a sleeping dog lie, so to speak, and stay away from the Word? Of course not! But do realize that while the difficulty for us in reading the Word of God may seem like it is mainly in issues of time or worldly things, the battles we fight in life are truly of a spiritual nature.

In the book of Ephesians (6:12), Paul tells us that ". . . our struggle is not against flesh and blood, but against the rulers, against the powers, against the world forces of this darkness, against the spiritual forces of wickedness in the heavenly places." It is for this reason that he goes on to tell us to arm ourselves with the full armor of God.

***Practical Point:* Put on the full armor of God**

Truth be told, when you start swinging the sword of the Spirit, it becomes evident to all that you are part of the active battle. The Word is the one offensive weapon we have on the battlefield (although it, too, is used defensively at times). Paul tells us about the equipment that we need to deal with as soldiers on this spiritual battlefield in Ephesians.

> *"Therefore, take up the full armor of God, so that you will be able to resist in the evil day, and having done everything, to stand firm. Stand firm therefore, HAVING GIRDED YOUR LOINS WITH TRUTH, and HAVING PUT ON THE BREASTPLATE OF RIGHTEOUSNESS, and having shod YOUR FEET WITH THE PREPARATION OF THE GOSPEL OF PEACE; in addition to all, taking up the shield of faith with which you will be able to extinguish all the flaming arrows of the evil one. And take the HELMET OF SALVATION, and the sword of the Spirit, which is the word of God."*
>
> *–Ephesians 6:13–17*

Although all analogies fall short at certain points, think for a moment with me of a football game. Eleven players from each side stand between the lines at any given point. More guys are members of the team, to be sure, but spend a good portion of the game sitting on the bench or roaming the sidelines. They're wearing their snazzy shirts and cute little pants, but as long as they're outside of the lines and not engaging the other team in battle, they really don't have to worry about getting clocked! Of course, they're not helping their own team either when they're outside the lines.

Anyone knowing an ounce about sports will understand the point here, OFFENSE DRAWS OPPOSITION. So when you pick up a weapon of offense spiritually, you must be wearing your defensive armor. A running back on a football team would never think of carrying the ball without wearing his helmet and other protective gear. Neither should you.

***Practical Point:* Decide even before you start that you will pursue God the hardest when you feel least like doing it**

You need to understand right up front that while reading through the Bible is totally within your grasp, it will not be easy sailing the whole way. Days will come when you feel distant from God. You may know why. You may not. You may be bored or tired or angry or frustrated or depressed. God may seem distant. Seek God in these times. Go to the Gospels, look at your Savior, and press on diligently as the author of Hebrews would exhort. When you feel most like pulling away, press in to God. Draw near the throne of grace. The author of Hebrews puts it so eloquently, explaining that in Jesus we have a merciful high priest who can sympathize with us because He too was a man:

> *"For we do not have a high priest who cannot sympathize with our weaknesses, but One who has been tempted in all things as we are, yet without sin. Therefore let us draw near with confidence to the throne of grace, so that we may receive mercy and find grace to help in time of need."*
>
> *–Hebrews 4:15–16*

***Practical Point:* Pursue God especially when you feel most distant and least worthy**

Ever make a big mistake? We all do. Maybe it was a moral slip-up. Maybe your mouth got the better of you. Maybe a bitter spirit has a grip over you. Maybe you just feel cheesed and you're not even sure why. Ever just feel distant? Whatever the case, when we fail God, we often just feel like avoiding Him. We feel like we are not worthy. Of course, apart from Christ, we aren't worthy. God knows our failures. Jesus understands our trials and temptations. He can sympathize. We need desperately to learn the four main exhortations of the book of Hebrews.

***Practical Point:* Learn the four exhortations of Hebrews: Consider Jesus, Hold Fast, Draw Near, Press On**

Consider Jesus:

Hebrews 3:1– "Therefore, holy brethren, partakers of a heavenly calling, ***consider Jesus****, the Apostle and High Priest of our confession . . . "*

Hold Fast:

Hebrews 3:6– ". . .but Christ was faithful as a Son over His house–whose house we are, if we ***hold fast*** *our confidence and the boast of our hope firm until the end."*

Hebrews 3:14– partakers of Christ, if we ***hold fast*** *the beginning of our assurance firm until the end . . ."*

Draw Near:

Hebrews 4:16– "Therefore let us ***draw near*** *with confidence to the throne of grace, so that we may receive mercy and find grace to help in time of need."*

Press On:

Hebrews 6:1– "Therefore leaving the elementary teaching about the Christ, let us ***press on*** *to maturity . . ."*

Boldface text shown above is mine.

Practical Point: ***Pray some more!***

Keep praying. Keep praying for the continued desire to read. Keep praying that God will open your eyes as you read to give you eyes that see and ears that hear. Pray every time you read. Prayer is so key, and yet it can be so easy to forget, especially if you are having success.

When we get clicking on all cylinders with God, it can be easy to forget what a gift it all is. Salvation is a gift, the faith to believe is a gift, the desire to read is a gift. None of it is of you, it is all of Him. Certainly we respond, but we need to always remember the source and to continue diligently in prayer as we grow.

Practical Point: ***Stop being afraid of the Bible***

Now if you're in the faint of heart category, which I sometimes (okay a lot of the times) am myself, you may be thinking, "Okay, if offense draws opposition, maybe I should just sit here on the sidelines. And after all, the Bible is a really long book and I probably wouldn't be able to finish it anyway, and if I did, what are the chances I'd be able to understand it?"

Let's be honest here; many adults are just plain afraid of the Bible. They're afraid they won't understand or they're afraid of the changes that they'll have to make if they do understand. I often wonder where in life it is that we pick up this pessimistic outlook. It must, however, be somewhere after the second grade.

A couple of weeks ago, while teaching a first and second grade Sunday School class, I explained to the kids that I was going to read the story right out of the Bible to show them that they could understand it right from the source, without me having to explain it or read it from a "kid Bible." I told them that I wanted to do this because many grown-ups think that the Bible is too hard to understand, but that I wanted them to grow up knowing the truth—they can understand the Bible.

They looked back at me incredulous! Grown-ups thinking the Bible was hard to understand? I must be kidding! I went on to read to them right out of the New Living Translation of the Bible, having to clarify only a couple of phrases along the way, and they answered all the questions I had for them. Too hard? No way, not with the right translation!

***Practical Point:* Find the right translation!**

We talked about it in the previous chapter, but the importance of this point begs another mention. Reading a translation that you can understand can make the difference between success and failure. If I had to venture a guess as to why many in the over-30 crowd think that reading through the Bible is just too hard, it would have to be that we were weaned on the King James Version of the Bible. Not that there's anything terribly theologically wrong with that version, particularly if you lived in the 1600s. We just don't talk the way that version was translated.

Fortunately for us, we have several excellent translations to choose from today. As mentioned earlier, I highly recommend the New Living Translation for first-time readers. The New International Version is also a very readable Bible. As we talked about in the last chapter, the New American Standard Bible remains the standard for Bible study, because of its word for word translation from the Greek text, but it can be harder when simply reading for general context. Eventually, do read through the New American Standard . . . it's still my favorite . . . just don't start there.

Practical Point: ***Don't worry that you're inadequate or not smart enough***

I wish that each person reading this book could meet a friend of mine. Her name is Michelle. She is one of my heroes. I first met Michelle several years ago when she was in her late teens. She is now 22 years old. Michelle is a special young lady. She has some learning disabilities. She doesn't drive. She works as an assistant activities coordinator at a long term care facility.

To speak casually with Michelle, you would never be able to guess what a student of the Bible she is. In fact, she has already read through the entire Bible in a year—several years earlier in her life than I did in mine! She has also attended a Precept Bible Study class (an in-depth study on Hebrews) for the past two years. For those not familiar with Precept studies, the studies require approximately five hours of homework each week in preparation for class time.

As I was chatting with Michelle the other night, she informed me that she had spent her afternoon on Sunday typing the rest of her class notes into her word processor. I was blown away. Like I said, she can't drive, but God has given Michelle the desire for His Word, and the degree of understanding that she needs. If each of us did with what we have what Michelle does with what she has, I'm convinced God would use us to turn the world upside down!

***Practical Point:* Realize that it is God who is doing the work in you**

In other words, don't even think about getting full of yourself. The book of Proverbs counsels that "Pride goes before destruction, And a haughty spirit before stumbling." As we make progress in reading through the Word, God will use it to change us from the inside out. The sin nature, however, still rears its head on occasion and tries to persuade us that we have made such spiritual progress because of our own hard work and superior skills. Baloney. It is by the grace of God that we are saved and it is by the grace of God that we have the power to persevere. Remember, once you've started looking at how cool you think you are, you've taken your eyes off of the goal, off of Jesus, and you're headed for trouble.

***Practical Point:* Focus on your mission; look to the goal, not to the obstacles**

Why do we spend so much more time looking at the obstacles instead of focusing on the goal? It's too hard, it's too long, I don't have the time. Stop it. Look to the goal of Jesus. When a runner competes in a race, he must fix his eyes on the goal. We must fix our eyes on Jesus as the author of Hebrews exhorts.

***Practical Point:* Move forward based on your faith and not your feelings**

I speak here to myself as much as anyone. Women especially need to hear this one. We are creatures of feelings. This is fine when we're talking about chick flicks and the like, but when we get to issues of faith, we can't let ourselves run on feelings or the adversary will deceive us every time. Satan is more powerful than you are on your own. No comparison. He is the father of lies and the schemes that he uses he uses on our minds. If he can use your feelings to deceive you, do you think he will? Absolutely. He doesn't play fair. That is why you need to know the full counsel of God. He does. And he'll twist it to suit his purpose in deceiving you every time if you let him.

Let's try this one on for size: Have you ever feared that you have committed the unpardonable sin that Jesus talks about, blasphemy against the Holy Spirit or that you are the man of Hebrews 6, the one of whom the writer says, "it is impossible to renew them again to repentance." You don't have to be a Bible teacher very long before one of these issues pops up. It is a common scheme of Satan's to make believers doubt their salvation. (And just for the record, biblical scholars overwhelmingly agree that if you're afraid that you've committed one of these sins, you haven't, because if you had, you wouldn't care!) These verses can be terrifying if taken out of the context of the whole. Whenever I have a scared student on my hands, I send them to the book of John, specifically chapter 10 which clearly teaches that of all that the Father has given to the Son, He will lose none. If this isn't assurance, I don't know what is.

Still, there are times we will not feel saved. We will be under attack. Guess what? If you're under attack, it is an evidence of the reality of the spiritual world. Our job? We are to stand firm in the faith (I Peter 5:9). God has not given us a spirit of fear, but one of power, and of love, and of a sound mind (II Timothy 1:7). He has given us weapons of warfare: defensive weapons and an offensive one, the sword of the Spirit, which is the Word of God.

Practical Point: ***Meet with Jesus every day!***

I had a theology professor in college who advised our class that no matter where we were reading in our Bibles, each one of us should meet with Jesus every day. Read even a few sentences from the Gospels when you're reading elsewhere in the Bible just to make sure that you are looking on the face of your Savior and Lord everyday. Do I always do this? No. I can tell you, though, that when the world is beating me down, and I need strength for my soul (and I'm thinking clearly enough), I run to the Gospels, because there is nothing like looking on the face of Jesus to quicken your spirit!

***Practical Point:* Realize that God looks for people with whole hearts to strongly support**

As I close this section, I'd like to leave you with some of the most encouraging words that I've found in the Bible. This may surprise you, but they come from the book of II Chronicles 16:9a:

> *"For the eyes of the LORD move to and fro throughout the earth that He may strongly support those whose heart is completely His."*

Final Challenge: On Your Mark, Get Set, Go!

Well, it's time to get going now. It's time to put down the how-to and start doing it. And doubtless there are some who still are skeptical, who still believe the lie that they can't do it. Remember, destructive thoughts like these come from our enemy. He is the father of lies and has lied from the beginning (John 8:44). Do you know how to combat lies? You combat them with the truth; the truth that is found in the Word of God. Is it any wonder that our enemy wants to keep us out of the Bible? As I said earlier, I find it very interesting that in the Garden of Eden the lie was, "You'll be as *smart* as God." Now the lie is, "You are so *dumb,* you'll never be able to understand the Bible."

For many of us, we have a tendency to have this odd fear of God, that if we sell out to Him 100% something bad is going to happen. We have to realize that He is

100% worthy of our trust. It makes no sense for us to trust Him with our eternity if we can't trust Him with our present lives. I have to admit, this is an area in which I struggle. There is a part of me that fears that if God is going to mold me, He is going to crush me and hurt me. Yet while this is what I fear, I know otherwise. While God may allow things into my life to shape me and conform me to the image of His Son, everything that enters my life is filtered through fingers of love. And not just any love, but a love that sacrificed all for me. He is not a malevolent deity. He is Abba; He is our Father, our Daddy. Our enemy would have us believe subtle lies—either that God is not totally in control, or that He is out to get us, or that if we give our all to Him, He will do us harm. These lies are for our mind. His schemes are for our mind. He is, according to Scripture, a roaring lion seeking to devour us. He is more powerful than we are, hands down. Without Christ, he can eat us alive, but in Christ there is no weapon formed against us that shall prosper, and even the gates of hell shall not prevail against our attacks.

We need the Word of God. We are in a war and His Word is our weapon; the sword of the Spirit is the Word of God. It is through His Word that we learn who He is, and what He calls us to be. We learn His promises, we learn how to pray, what to pray for, what kinds of prayers He answers. We learn of our sinfulness and His holiness.

We learn just how much He loves us and how He wants us to live.

So when we pare it all down, we are left with the question:

To whom will you listen?

Will you listen to the voice of God who wants only the best for you or will you listen to the voice of the enemy of your soul?

Choose God. Choose today!

Appendix A: The Text of I John

from the New American Standard Bible

Chapter 1

1 What was from the beginning, what we have heard,
what we have seen with our eyes, what we beheld and
our hands handled, concerning the Word of Life– 2 and
the life was manifested, and we have seen and bear wit-
ness and proclaim to you the eternal life, which was with
the Father and was manifested to us– 3 what we have
seen and heard we proclaim to you also, that you also
may have fellowship with us; and indeed our fellowship
is with the Father, and with His Son Jesus Christ. 4 And
these things we write, so that our joy may be made com-
plete. 5 And this is the message we have heard from Him

and announce to you, that God is light, and in Him there
is no darkness at all. 6 If we say that we have fellowship
with Him and [yet] walk in the darkness, we lie and do
not practice the truth; 7 but if we walk in the light as He
Himself is in the light, we have fellowship with one anoth-
er, and the blood of Jesus His Son cleanses us from all sin.
8 If we say that we have no sin, we are deceiving our-
selves, and the truth is not in us. 9 If we confess our sins,
He is faithful and righteous to forgive us our sins and to
cleanse us from all unrighteousness. 10 If we say that we
have not sinned, we make Him a liar, and His word is not
in us.

Chapter 2

1 My little children, I am writing these things to you
that you may not sin. And if anyone sins, we have an
Advocate with the Father, Jesus Christ the righteous; 2
and He Himself is the propitiation for our sins; and not
for ours only, but also for [those of] the whole world. 3
And by this we know that we have come to know Him, if
we keep His commandments. 4 The one who says, "I
have come to know Him," and does not keep His com-
mandments, is a liar, and the truth is not in him; 5 but
whoever keeps His word, in him the love of God has truly
been perfected. By this we know that we are in Him: 6
the one who says he abides in Him ought himself to walk
in the same manner as He walked. 7 Beloved, I am not
writing a new commandment to you, but an old com-

mandment which you have had from the beginning; the
old commandment is the word which you have heard. 8
On the other hand, I am writing a new commandment to
you, which is true in Him and in you, because the dark-
ness is passing away, and the true light is already shining.
9 The one who says he is in the light and [yet] hates his
brother is in the darkness until now. 10 The one who
loves his brother abides in the light and there is no cause
for stumbling in him. 11 But the one who hates his broth-
er is in the darkness and walks in the darkness, and does
not know where he is going because the darkness has
blinded his eyes. 12 I am writing to you, little children,
because your sins are forgiven you for His name's sake.
13 I am writing to you, fathers, because you know Him
who has been from the beginning. I am writing to you,
young men, because you have overcome the evil one. I
have written to you, children, because you know the
Father. 14 I have written to you, fathers, because you
know Him who has been from the beginning. I have writ-
ten to you, young men, because you are strong, and the
word of God abides in you, and you have overcome the
evil one. 15 Do not love the world, nor the things in the
world. If anyone loves the world, the love of the Father is
not in him. 16 For all that is in the world, the lust of the
flesh and the lust of the eyes and the boastful pride of life,
is not from the Father, but is from the world. 17 And the
world is passing away, and [also] its lusts; but the one

who does the will of God abides forever. 18 Children, it
is the last hour; and just as you heard that antichrist is
coming, even now many antichrists have arisen; from this
we know that it is the last hour. 19 They went out from
us, but they were not [really] of us; for if they had been of
us, they would have remained with us; but [they went
out,] in order that it might be shown that they all are not
of us. 20 But you have an anointing from the Holy One,
and you all know. 21 I have not written to you because
you do not know the truth, but because you do know it,
and because no lie is of the truth. 22 Who is the liar but
the one who denies that Jesus is the Christ? This is the
antichrist, the one who denies the Father and the Son. 23
Whoever denies the Son does not have the Father; the
one who confesses the Son has the Father also. 24 As for
you, let that abide in you which you heard from the
beginning. If what you heard from the beginning abides
in you, you also will abide in the Son and in the Father. 25
And this is the promise which He Himself made to us:
eternal life. 26 These things I have written to you con-
cerning those who are trying to deceive you. 27 And as
for you, the anointing which you received from Him
abides in you, and you have no need for anyone to teach
you; but as His anointing teaches you about all things,
and is true and is not a lie, and just as it has taught you,
you abide in Him. 28 And now, little children, abide in
Him, so that when He appears, we may have confidence

and not shrink away from Him in shame at His coming.
29 If you know that He is righteous, you know that every-
one also who practices righteousness is born of Him.

Chapter 3

1 See how great a love the Father has bestowed upon
us, that we should be called children of God; and [such]
we are. For this reason the world does not know us,
because it did not know Him. 2 Beloved, now we are
children of God, and it has not appeared as yet what we
shall be. We know that, when He appears, we shall be like
Him, because we shall see Him just as He is. 3 And every-
one who has this hope [fixed] on Him purifies himself,
just as He is pure. 4 Everyone who practices sin also
practices lawlessness; and sin is lawlessness. 5 And you
know that He appeared in order to take away sins; and in
Him there is no sin. 6 No one who abides in Him sins;
no one who sins has seen Him or knows Him. 7 Little
children, let no one deceive you; the one who practices
righteousness is righteous, just as He is righteous; 8 the
one who practices sin is of the devil; for the devil has
sinned from the beginning. The Son of God appeared for
this purpose, that He might destroy the works of the
devil. 9 No one who is born of God practices sin,
because His seed abides in him; and he cannot sin,
because he is born of God. 10 By this the children of
God and the children of the devil are obvious: anyone
who does not practice righteousness is not of God, nor

the one who does not love his brother. 11 For this is the
message which you have heard from the beginning, that
we should love one another; 12 not as Cain, [who] was
of the evil one, and slew his brother. And for what reason
did he slay him? Because his deeds were evil, and his
brother's were righteous. 13 Do not marvel, brethren, if
the world hates you. 14 We know that we have passed
out of death into life, because we love the brethren. He
who does not love abides in death. 15 Everyone who
hates his brother is a murderer; and you know that no
murderer has eternal life abiding in him. 16 We know
love by this, that He laid down His life for us; and we
ought to lay down our lives for the brethren. 17 But who-
ever has the world's goods, and beholds his brother in
need and closes his heart against him, how does the love
of God abide in him? 18 Little children, let us not love
with word or with tongue, but in deed and truth. 19 We
shall know by this that we are of the truth, and shall
assure our heart before Him, 20 in whatever our heart
condemns us; for God is greater than our heart, and
knows all things. 21 Beloved, if our heart does not con-
demn us, we have confidence before God; 22 and what-
ever we ask we receive from Him, because we keep His
commandments and do the things that are pleasing in
His sight. 23 And this is His commandment, that we
believe in the name of His Son Jesus Christ, and love one
another, just as He commanded us. 24 And the one who

keeps His commandments abides in Him, and He in him.
And we know by this that He abides in us, by the Spirit
whom He has given us.

Chapter 4

1 Beloved, do not believe every spirit, but test the
spirits to see whether they are from God; because many
false prophets have gone out into the world. 2 By this
you know the Spirit of God: every spirit that confesses
that Jesus Christ has come in the flesh is from God; 3 and
every spirit that does not confess Jesus is not from God;
and this is the [spirit] of the antichrist, of which you have
heard that it is coming, and now it is already in the world.
4 You are from God, little children, and have overcome
them; because greater is He who is in you than he who is
in the world. 5 They are from the world; therefore they
speak [as] from the world, and the world listens to them.
6 We are from God; he who knows God listens to us; he
who is not from God does not listen to us. By this we
know the spirit of truth and the spirit of error. 7 Beloved,
let us love one another, for love is from God; and every-
one who loves is born of God and knows God. 8 The
one who does not love does not know God, for God is
love. 9 By this the love of God was manifested in us, that
God has sent His only begotten Son into the world so that
we might live through Him. 10 In this is love, not that we
loved God, but that He loved us and sent His Son [to be]
the propitiation for our sins. 11 Beloved, if God so loved

us, we also ought to love one another. 12 No one has beheld God at any time; if we love one another, God abides in us, and His love is perfected in us. 13 By this we know that we abide in Him and He in us, because He has given us of His Spirit. 14 And we have beheld and bear witness that the Father has sent the Son [to be] the Savior of the world. 15 Whoever confesses that Jesus is the Son of God, God abides in him, and he in God. 16 And we have come to know and have believed the love which God has for us. God is love, and the one who abides in love abides in God, and God abides in him. 17 By this, love is perfected with us, that we may have confidence in the day of judgment; because as He is, so also are we in this world. 18 There is no fear in love; but perfect love casts out fear, because fear involves punishment, and the one who fears is not perfected in love. 19 We love, because He first loved us. 20 If someone says, "I love God," and hates his brother, he is a liar; for the one who does not love his brother whom he has seen, cannot love God whom he has not seen. 21 And this commandment we have from Him, that the one who loves God should love his brother also.

Chapter 5

1 Whoever believes that Jesus is the Christ is born of God; and whoever loves the Father loves the [child] born of Him. 2 By this we know that we love the children of God, when we love God and observe His command-

ments. 3 For this is the love of God, that we keep His
commandments; and His commandments are not bur-
densome. 4 For whatever is born of God overcomes the
world; and this is the victory that has overcome the
world— our faith. 5 And who is the one who overcomes
the world, but he who believes that Jesus is the Son of
God? 6 This is the one who came by water and blood,
Jesus Christ; not with the water only, but with the water
and with the blood. 7 And it is the Spirit who bears wit-
ness, because the Spirit is the truth. 8 For there are three
that bear witness, the Spirit and the water and the blood;
and the three are in agreement. 9 If we receive the wit-
ness of men, the witness of God is greater; for the witness
of God is this, that He has borne witness concerning His
Son. 10 The one who believes in the Son of God has the
witness in himself; the one who does not believe God has
made Him a liar, because he has not believed in the wit-
ness that God has borne concerning His Son. 11 And the
witness is this, that God has given us eternal life, and this
life is in His Son. 12 He who has the Son has the life; he
who does not have the Son of God does not have the life.
13 These things I have written to you who believe in the
name of the Son of God, in order that you may know that
you have eternal life. 14 And this is the confidence which
we have before Him, that, if we ask anything according to
His will, He hears us. 15 And if we know that He hears us
[in] whatever we ask, we know that we have the requests

which we have asked from Him. 16 If anyone sees his brother committing a sin not [leading] to death, he shall ask and [God] will for him give life to those who commit sin not [leading] to death. There is a sin [leading] to death; I do not say that he should make request for this. 17 All unrighteousness is sin, and there is a sin not [leading] to death. 18 We know that no one who is born of God sins; but He who was born of God keeps him and the evil one does not touch him. 19 We know that we are of God, and the whole world lies in [the power of] the evil one. 20 And we know that the Son of God has come, and has given us understanding, in order that we might know Him who is true, and we are in Him who is true, in His Son Jesus Christ. This is the true God and eternal life. 21 Little children, guard yourselves from idols.

Appendix B: Helpful Books

Bible Study Books:

How to Read the Bible for All its Worth, by G. Fee and D. Stuart;
Grand Rapids, Michigan: Zondervan, 1993.

How to Study Your Bible, by Kay Arthur;
Eugene, Oregon: Harvest House Publishers, 1994.

Other Helpful Books:

Celebration of Discipline, by Richard J. Foster;
San Francisco, California: Harper & Row Publishers, 1978.

The Cost of Discipleship, by Dietrich Bonhoeffer;
New York, New York: Simon & Schuster, 1995.

The Spirit of the Disciplines, by Dallas Willard;
San Francisco, California: HarperSanfrancisco, 1988.

Reference Works:

The Complete Word Study Dictionary: New Testament, by Spiros Zodhiates; Chattanooga, Tennessee: AMG Publishers, 1992.

The Complete Word Study Dictionary: Old Testament, by Spiros Zodhiates; Chattanooga, Tennessee: AMG Publishers, 1993.

New International Dictionary of New Testament Theology, 4 volumes, edited by Colin Brown; Grand Rapids, Michigan: Zondervan, 1986.

Strong's Exhaustive Concordance of the Bible, by James Strong; McLean, Virginia: MacDonald Publishing Company.

Theological Dictionary of the New Testament Abridged, edited by Geoffrey W. Bromiley; Grand Rapids, Michigan: Eerdmans, 1985.

Theological Word Book of the Old Testament, 2 volumes, edited by L.R. Harris; G.L. Archer, Jr.; and B.K. Waltke; Chicago, Illinois: Moody Press, 1980.

Vine's Complete Expository Dictionary of Old and New Testament Words, edited by W.E. Vine, M.F. Unger, and W. White; New York, New York: Thomas Nelson Publishers, 1985.

Appendix C: Bible Study Information

For more information on Bible studies in your area, contact the organizations listed below.

Precept Ministries International
7324 Noah Reid Road
P.O. Box 182218
Chattanooga, Tennessee 37422
Toll Free: 800/763-8280
Fax: 423/894-2449
www.precept.org

Living Proof Ministries (Beth Moore Studies)
5870 Highway 6 North, Suite 307
Houston, Texas 77084
281/859-1375
Fax: 281/859-3610
www.lproof.org

Bible Study Fellowship International
19001 Huebner Road
San Antonio, Texas 78258
210/492-4676
Fax: 210/493-4111
Toll Free Class Information Line: 877/273-3228
www.bsfinternational.org

Appendix D: Quick Book Summaries

Whatever you do, don't read these quickie summaries and think you've got yourself a handle on the whole Bible! Remember, I'm not a PhD, ThD or any other "D"! I'm still a learner myself. So, from one learner to another, here are some observations on what you'll find in the books of the Bible, and if the books are "easy" to read, "moderate" in difficulty, or just plain "difficult" on the subjective Pam-scale. Remember, "difficult" doesn't mean you can't understand them, just that they might not be crystal clear the first (or second) time around, and "easy" doesn't mean that there won't be any sticky issues of interpretation or application!

Old Testament

The Books of the Law

Genesis – Starts with the creation of the universe, animals, and mankind. Major storyline follows the lives of Adam, Noah, Abraham, Isaac, Jacob, and Joseph. 50 chapters. Easy reading.

Exodus – Begins in Egypt with a new king (pharaoh) coming to power who did not know Joseph and what he had done for Egypt. Tells of the enslavement of the Israelites and their eventual exodus (leaving) from Egypt by the power of God. The main human character in the book is Moses. In Exodus we have the giving of the Law at Mt. Sinai and the institution of the Tabernacle with a great deal of instructions relating to it, its contents, and the priests. The low point of the book is the making of the golden calf while Moses is receiving the Law from God. 40 chapters. Moderate reading.

Leviticus – Rules and regulations for Israel! What sacrifices were required? What was required of the priest? Of the people? In the book of Leviticus we see what was required of a sinful people in the presence of a holy God. This book is often the undoing of people who try to read through the Bible in a linear fashion. 27 chapters. Difficult reading.

Numbers - Yes, Numbers has lots of numbers as the people are "numbered" by tribe and more instructions are given on sacrifices and offerings. But for a book that starts off with less than a bang, Numbers boasts some extremely memorable accounts from the wilderness wanderings, including Miriam (the sister of Moses) being struck with leprosy, Israel sending the spies into the promised land, and Korah, a rebellious Levite, being swallowed alive by the ground (bet you never heard that story in Sunday School!). Numbers also includes such memorable stories as the bronze serpent in the wilderness and the talking donkey of Balaam. 36 chapters. Moderate reading.

Deuteronomy - Moses' life is drawing to a close and the children of Israel are just about to enter the promised land under the leadership of Joshua. With this background, Moses speaks to Israel reminding them of the works of God and calling them to obedience to the covenant and laying out for them the blessings and curses associated with keeping or breaking the covenant. After giving the commands to Israel on the east side of the Jordan River, Moses dies at the end of the book, being remembered in Deuteronomy 34:10b as one whom "the Lord knew face to face." 34 chapters. Moderate reading.

History

Joshua - What an AWESOME book! God leads Joshua (the successor to Moses) and the people of Israel across the parted Jordan River and into the land which He had promised to Abraham way back in Genesis. In this historical book we find the familiar stories of Rahab the harlot and the toppling of the walls of Jericho. We also meet the incredible spy, Caleb, who followed the Lord fully! Throughout the book we see both the results of obedience and the results of sinful actions. 24 chapters. Easy reading (with the exception of a few chapters on the division of the land among the tribes of Israel).

Judges - After the death of Joshua, individual judges raised up by God lead the people of Israel. Judges is a book of cycles. The people forget God and sin against Him. God brings judgment against them in the form of oppression from another nation. When the people wake up and cry out to God for help, God sends a deliverer for them. They typically behave well enough while the judge is alive and then upon the death of the judge fall away and get thumped again. Some of the more memorable judges include Deborah, Gideon, and Samson. 21 chapters. Easy reading.

Ruth - Biography of Ruth, a Moabite woman who becomes part of the line of Christ. Her faithfulness to her

Israelite mother-in-law Naomi is legendary. Ruth marries the son of Naomi when Naomi, her husband and two sons comes to live in the land of Moab during a famine in Israel. While in Moab, Naomi's husband dies. Later, when both of her sons die, she decides to return to Israel. Ruth insists on going with her and the rest is history. 4 chapters. Easy reading.

I Samuel - The book begins with the life of Samuel, the last judge in Israel, and ends with the life and death of Saul, the first king in Israel. Although mentioned in the lineage in the book of Ruth, David makes his first appearance in I Samuel. He kills Goliath, strikes up a friendship with Jonathan (King Saul's son), and spends much of the book fleeing from King Saul. 31 chapters. Easy reading.

II Samuel - II Samuel follows the ascension to power and life of King David. It includes the story of David and Bathsheba, and the death of David's son Absalom. Ending on an uncharacteristic low note in David's life (right down there, so to speak, with the Bathsheba event), the book draws to a close with the wrath of God being poured out against Israel in the form of pestilence in the land for three days as a result of David's sin of taking a census and numbering the people. 24 chapters. Easy reading.

I Kings - Beginning with the death of King David, I Kings follows the kingdom of Israel under David's son, King Solomon as he asks wisdom of God and subsequently builds the Temple at Jerusalem. In spite of all his wisdom, Solomon allows foreign women and their gods to turn his heart from the Lord. Because of this, God divides the kingdom under Solomon's arrogant son, Rehoboam, leaving David's line to rule the Southern Kingdom of two tribes (Judah and Benjamin) often called Judah. The Northern Kingdom of the other ten tribes retains the name Israel. The remainder of the book tells of the exploits of the kings of Judah and Israel, as well as accounts of the prophets Elijah and Elisha. The book ends with the account of King Ahaziah in Israel and the content continues right into the beginning of II Kings. 22 chapters. Easy reading.

II Kings - A continuation of I Kings, this book follows the kings and kingdom of Israel up to their defeat and deportation by Assyria in 722 BC, and follows Judah to the time of the Babylonian captivity in 586 BC. The taking up of Elijah and the ministry of Elisha are also covered in II Kings. 25 chapters. Easy reading.

I Chronicles - Heavy on the genealogies for the first nine chapters, then moves into chronicling the life of King David for much of the book. 29 chapters. Difficult reading in chapters 1-9 and 23-27. Easy reading remainder of book.

II Chronicles - Beginning with Solomon and the building of the Temple, II Chronicles tells of the subsequent kings of Israel and Judah, following Judah all the way to the time of Cyrus king of Persia. It was Persia that had conquered the Babylonian Empire. Judah had been taken into captivity in Babylon in 586 BC. 36 chapters. Moderate reading.

Ezra - Ezra continues the historical account, picking up the story of the people of Judah who are in captivity in Babylon and how a group is sent back to Jerusalem by King Cyrus of Persia to rebuild the Temple. 10 chapters. Moderate reading.

Nehemiah - The book of Nehemiah tells of the reconstructing of the wall of Jerusalem and the renewing of the covenant after the Babylonian exile. 13 chapters. Moderate reading.

Esther - This book tells the story of Queen Esther, a Jewess who unwittingly became Queen of Persia and saved her people from extermination at the hands of the wicked Haman. 10 chapters. Easy reading.

Poetry and Wisdom Literature

Job – Why do bad things happen to good people? Even people who don't read the Bible know what it means to suffer like Job. This godly man loses everything, but remains faithful to God through severe trials and tragedies. In the end, God restores his health and possessions, but it is a long time in coming. 42 chapters. Difficult reading.

Psalms – What a book of worship, this song book of Israel! King David wrote many of the psalms and as you read, you'll recognize that many of our current worship songs are lifted directly from this portion of the Bible. 150 chapters. Easy reading.

Proverbs – While many of the psalms are attributed to David, his son, Solomon wrote much of Proverbs. The Proverbs give practical advice on living, not promises per se, but the results that generally follow from a given set of actions. 31 chapters. Easy reading.

Ecclesiastes – Written by Solomon, a man who had everything, Ecclesiastes concludes that all life has to offer apart from God is vanity. 12 chapters. Moderate reading.

Song of Solomon – A love story written by Solomon. Shows the high biblical view of physical love within marriage. Not a good place to start your children reading the Bible. 8 chapters. Moderate reading.

Major Prophets

Isaiah - Writing to the Southern Kingdom of Judah before they are taken into captivity by Babylon, Isaiah not only warns of coming judgment, but also has much to say about the coming Messiah and the millennial kingdom. Tradition says that Isaiah was eventually martyred by being sawn in two. 66 chapters. Difficult reading.

Jeremiah - Jeremiah also prophesied to Judah, but after the time of Isaiah. Jeremiah is often referred to as the weeping prophet. He continually characterizes Judah as having stiff necks and ears that will not listen. They are stubborn with evil hearts. Yet we have in this prophet the view toward the New Covenant when God will write His laws on the hearts of His people (Jeremiah 31) and cause them to walk in His ways. 52 chapters. Difficult reading.

Lamentations - Generally attributed to Jeremiah, the book of Lamentations laments the fall of Jerusalem to Babylon. 5 chapters. Moderate reading.

Ezekiel - Ezekiel prophesied to the people of Judah who had been taken into captivity in Babylon. This book features great visions of God, but the end of the book is very difficult to wade through as it is a very detailed description of a yet future Temple, probably during the millennial kingdom. 48 chapters. Difficult reading.

Daniel - Taken into captivity in Babylon during his youth, Daniel rose to power under different leaders, but never compromised in his unswerving devotion to his God. The book of Daniel contains some difficult prophetic sections, in addition to the well-known stories of Daniel in the Lion's Den and Shadrach, Meshach, and Abednego in the fiery furnace. 12 chapters. Mixture of easy and difficult reading.

Minor Prophets

Hosea - Don't like your job? Just consider the job this guy is given. God tells Hosea to marry a prostitute as a picture of God's faithful love to Israel even though she is continually unfaithful to Him. Hosea prophesied to the Northern Kingdom of Israel. 14 chapters. Moderate reading.

Joel - Joel writes to Judah, the Southern Kingdom, prior to the Babylonian captivity and speaks of locusts, destruction, and ultimate deliverance. 3 chapters. Moderate reading.

Amos - A shepherd from Judah, Amos was sent to prophesy to the Northern Kingdom of Israel prior to their fall to Assyria. 9 chapters. Moderate reading.

Obadiah - Obadiah prophesies against the descendants of Esau, the people of Edom. 1 chapter. Moderate reading.

Jonah - Jonah, probably the most famous of the minor prophets, is sent not to the people of Israel or Judah, but to the wicked city of Ninevah. When he decides not to do his job, Jonah is swallowed by a great fish before he finally repents and delivers the message God has for him to give. 4 chapters. Easy reading.

Micah - Micah of Moresheth prophesied to Judah well before the Babylonian captivity. He speaks of coming judgment, but also of a coming ruler "From the days of eternity," who will go forth from Bethlehem. Hmm, wonder who that could be?! 7 chapters. Moderate reading.

Nahum - Nahum prophesies to Judah, the Southern Kingdom, prior to the Babylonian captivity. His message is the coming judgment against Ninevah, the capital of the mighty Assyrian Empire that had conquered the Northern Kingdom of Israel. 3 chapters. Moderate reading.

Habakkuk - Habakkuk prophesies to Judah of the impending judgment coming at the hand of Babylon. He questions why God is using evil Babylon to judge His people. 3 chapters. Moderate reading.

Zephaniah - Another prophet to Judah, Zephaniah also spoke of the coming judgment by Babylon, yet looks forward to the blessings of the millennial kingdom. 3 chapters. Moderate reading.

Haggai - Haggai wrote after the Babylonian exile to call the people to finish the reconstruction of the Temple. 2 chapters. Moderate reading.

Zechariah - Like Haggai, Zechariah called the people to finish rebuilding the Temple. Zechariah is filled with many references to the coming Messiah. 14 chapters. Moderate reading.

Malachi - Malachi wrote after the people had returned from captivity to their homeland. Apparently conquest by their enemies was far enough in the past that the people were once again drifting away from God. 4 chapters. Moderate reading.

New Testament

The Gospels

Matthew, Mark, and Luke are often termed the Synoptic Gospels. They each chronicle the life of Jesus Christ, but aim at different audiences. In the Synoptics, some accounts are recorded by all three evangelists, some by two, others by only one of the three.

Matthew - Matthew wrote to a Jewish audience. The Sermon on the Mount appears in Matthew 5-7. Much of Jesus' teaching in this Gospel has to do with what the kingdom of God is like. It is like a mustard seed, like leaven, like a treasure hidden in a field. 28 chapters. Easy reading.

Mark - Mark wrote to a Roman audience. He also wrote, by far, the shortest of the Gospel accounts. 16 chapters. Easy reading.

Luke - Luke, the physician, wrote to "Theophillus," his Greek, Gentile friend. Luke is also the author of the book of Acts. Luke features the Christmas story that may be read at your house on Christmas Eve (it always is at mine) that is found in Luke 2:1-20. Also notable in Luke is the story of Zaccheus (the wee little man). 24 chapters. Easy reading.

John - John the Apostle takes a different approach in writing his Gospel. He tells us that he has written "that you may believe that Jesus is the Christ, the Son of God; and that believing, you may have life in His name." (John 20:31b) Unlike the Synoptic Gospels that take a more chronological approach, John's outline follows seven major signs performed by Jesus. Twenty-wonderful chapters. Easy reading.

The History of the Early Church

Acts - In Acts, Luke, the author of the Gospel bearing his name, recounts the birth of the Church. He tells of the ascension of Christ, the coming of the Holy Spirit, the martyrdom of Stephen, the preaching of Peter, and the conversion and subsequent ministry of Paul. 28 chapters. Easy reading.

The Epistles (Letters)

Romans - In his most thorough discussion of doctrine, Paul explains the righteousness of God in the letter to the Romans. Excellent book to ground new Christians. 16 chapters. Moderate reading.

I Corinthians - You think your church has problems? The church at Corinth had issues out the ears! In this letter, Paul discusses such issues as divisions in the church, problems of gross immorality, marriage and divorce, as well as other topics. 16 chapters. Easy reading.

II Corinthians - Really, you have to figure a church with as many problems as Corinth was going to take more than one letter! 13 chapters. Easy reading.

Galatians - Confused on the relationship of the Christian to the Law? Galatians is the book for you! Often considered a mini -Romans, Paul emphasizes that the way to God is through faith alone, not working your way to

Him. This is the book where you'll find the fruit of the Spirit listed. 6 chapters. Easy reading.

Ephesians - Paul writes the church at Ephesus telling them who they are "in Christ," and what this means as they live their lives. 6 chapters. Easy reading.

Philippians - In the letter to the Philippians, Paul covers topics including joy, unity, and humility. 4 chapters. Easy reading.

Colossians - Need to brush up on the person and work of Jesus Christ? Soak in Colossians for a couple of weeks! 4 chapters. Easy reading.

I Thessalonians - Unlike the Corinthian church, the church at Thessalonica was apparently "doing the job," and Paul tells them to "excel still more." In addition to other topics, Paul addresses the question of the Day of the Lord. 5 chapters. Easy reading.

II Thessalonians - Paul spends much of this epistle setting people straight on the Day of the Lord. 3 chapters. Moderate reading.

I Timothy - Paul packs a number of 21st century issues in this one as he addresses the topics of church leadership and women in the church. 6 chapters. Easy reading.

II Timothy - Just before his martyr's death, Paul writes to his son in the faith, Timothy, to pass the baton and remind him to guard the Gospel with which he has been entrusted, and to pass it along to faithful men who will be able to teach others also. 4 chapters. Easy reading.

Titus - Paul writes to tell Titus to exhort the church in sound doctrine and to engage in good deeds. He is to appoint elders and instruct those in the church on how to live in a manner that honors Christ. 3 chapters. Easy reading.

Philemon - This is a personal letter from Paul to Philemon regarding his runaway slave Onesimus, who had come to faith in Christ. 1 chapter. Easy reading.

Hebrews - The author of Hebrews exhorts what is probably a primarily Jewish church facing persecution to consider Jesus, its merciful and faithful high priest who is able to save forever. Knowing this, they are to hold fast, to draw near, and to press on to maturity. 13 chapters. Some difficult subject matter, but wonderful reading.

James - I always get a good "toe-steppin'" from the book of James. Sure, the first thing that many associate with James is the concept of faith and works, but it's always the teaching on the tongue that has me confessing. 5 chapters. Easy reading.

I Peter - The Apostle Peter speaks of topics including the relationship of the husband and wife, and the issue of suffering in the lives of those who follow Christ. 5 chapters. Easy reading.

II Peter - In a letter that has many similarities to Jude's, Peter stresses the concept of true knowledge of God in the face of false teachers. 3 chapters. Easy reading.

I John - Wondering if you really have eternal life? Read I John; that's why the Apostle John wrote this letter. 5 chapters. Easy reading (even in Greek!).

II John - In this short letter, John talks about walking in the truth and abiding in the teaching of Christ. 1 chapter. Easy reading.

III John - This is a personal letter from the Apostle John to a man named Gaius dealing with a specific problem in the church. 1 chapter. Easy reading.

Jude - Jude, the half-brother of Jesus, writes to tell the church to contend earnestly for the faith. He warns of coming judgment citing numerous Old Testament examples, yet assures that God is able to keep them from stumbling and to make them stand before His presence blameless with great joy. 1 chapter. Moderate reading.

Prophecy

Revelation - The Apostle John writes a prophetic book that has yet to see its ultimate fulfillment. Awesome pictures of heaven and exhortations to endure. Do I understand it all? No. Do I love it? Yes. By the way, I hear the Precept courses on Revelation are excellent! 22 chapters. Difficult reading, but worthwhile if for no other reason (and there are many other reasons) than to see the descriptions of the throne of God and of heaven.

Just in case you're chicken, let me whet your appetite:

> *"And I saw no temple in it, for the Lord God, the Almighty, and the Lamb, are its temple. And the city has no need of the sun or of the moon to shine upon it, for the glory of God has illumined it, and its lamp is the Lamb."*
>
> *–Revelation 21:22–23*

Appendix E: A Five-Minute Summary of the Old Testament

In the beginning God creates. Adam is the first man created, Eve the first woman. They are created by God without sin, but are quickly deceived in the Garden of Eden by the serpent (later identified as Satan). Eve actually eats the forbidden fruit (from the tree of the knowledge of good and evil) first and gives it to her husband Adam. Through this act of sin, death enters the world. Adam and Eve are banished from the beautiful garden so they cannot eat of the tree of life, and therefore live eternally in a state of alienation from God.

Although man rebels against God, God immediately predicts the coming of a Savior who will crush the head of the serpent (Messianic Covenant). This prophecy is later fulfilled in the person of Jesus Christ. However, in the meantime, sin has entered into the world, and death through sin.

Adam and Eve have many children; the most famous of them are the first two, Cain and Abel. Cain, resentful that God had accepted Abel's sacrifice and not his own, kills Abel, and sin really starts rolling. Things continue to go downhill from here until God has simply had enough. Saying that He regrets having made man, God calls Noah to build an ark so He can save him and his family from the coming destruction of the world by means of a flood. Noah obeys and God saves him, his wife, and his three sons and their wives. After the flood, God puts a rainbow in the sky as a sign of His covenant with all living creatures that He will never again destroy the entire earth with a flood.

Noah's sons, Japheth, Shem, and Ham become the fathers of all the nations. Over time, the population of the world increases and the people again begin to go off course when in their pride they determine to build a tower that will reach to heaven. In the midst of the construction, God confuses their languages, thereby thwarting their plans.

The next major player on the scene is Abraham, originally known as Abram. Abram and his wife Sarai (whose name is later changed to Sarah) live in the land of Ur. God tells Abram that he must leave the land that he is living in to go to a land that God will show him. Abram trusts God and goes, taking with him his wife and household. Although God changes his name to Abraham and promises to make him a great nation, Abraham finds himself really old with no children.

Taking matters into her own hands, Sarah decides to play God. She gives her handmaiden Hagar to Abraham so that the promise might be fulfilled through her seed on behalf of Sarah. Not a good idea. Hagar bears Abraham a son named Ishmael and Sarah is steamed.

Eventually, God does bless Sarah with a son in her old age. His name is Isaac and it is through him that God chooses to fulfill His promise to Abraham.

Like his father before him, Isaac finds himself in possession of a promise to be a great nation, but without a child for quite some time. Isaac, though, prays for his wife Rebekah and God causes her to conceive twins, Esau and Jacob.

These babies certainly weren't twins of the identical variety, Esau being a tough, manly man though an aisle shy in the brains department, while Jacob was an instigating, conniving, mama's boy. Although older, Esau lost both his birthright and blessing due to the trickery of his younger brother. Let's just say it's a good thing that they didn't have to look across the table at each other at Christmas dinner.

Warts and all, Jacob is God's chosen brother. Any guesses as to what Jacob's name becomes? That's right, Israel! Hence, the nation of Israel. See, this isn't so hard, is it? Rather appropriately, Jacob ends up with an extra wife after his uncle (also his new father-in-law) pulls a wedding day bait-and-switch on him. Thus, from Jacob, his wives Leah and Rachel, and their handmaidens (read "baby wars") are born what we know as the twelve tribes of Israel.

The most famous of Jacob's children is his son Joseph, the guy with the amazing Technicolor dreamcoat. His father's favorite, Joseph was sold by his brothers into slavery in Egypt. Eventually, God raises Joseph up to second in command in all of Egypt. He is reunited with his family who then come to live with him in Egypt.

After Joseph dies, everything is still fine until eventually a Pharaoh rises to power who does not remember Joseph and the way God used him to save Egypt. This Pharaoh decides to enslave the family of Joseph, now called the Hebrews, who have grown to great numbers in the land. The Hebrews remain in bondage for 400 years until the time of Moses.

Because the Hebrew population in Egypt has grown so rapidly, the Egyptian Pharaoh issues a decree that all male Hebrew babies should be killed. He fears that the slaves may turn against him should a foreign country invade. During this time, the mother of Moses hides her newborn son in a basket and sets it in the river to save him. The Pharaoh's daughter sees the basket with the infant and adopts him, raising him as her own. As an adult, young Moses intervenes in a fight between an Egyptian and one of his Hebrew brothers, killing the Egyptian. He subsequently flees Egypt and becomes a shepherd for 40 years until God calls to him from a burning bush to go back and deliver the Hebrews from Egypt.

Although resistant at first, Moses eventually obeys and after a series of 10 plagues and the Passover, he leads the Hebrews out of Egypt and on their way to the promised land. On the way, God parts the Red Sea, He feeds them with manna, and leads them with a cloud by day and a pillar of fire at night. Although they get to the promised land quickly, 10 of the 12 spies sent into the land report that giants occupy the land. They shrink back in fear instead of trusting God's promise. Thus, God makes them wander in the wilderness for 40 years before they are finally allowed to enter the promised land.

Moses sees the promised land from afar, but it is Joshua who leads the people into the promised land. Under his leadership, the famed walls of Jericho fall and the people, more or less, follow God. When Joshua dies, however, the people return to their wandering ways, having not driven out all of the people from the lands that they had conquered.

Into this rebellious situation, God sends the judges to help save the people when they call out to Him for help.

Some of the more notable judges include Deborah, Gideon, Samson, and Samuel.

During the time of Samuel, however, the people of Israel cry out for a king so they will be like the other nations around them. Bad move. By asking for a king, God says they are in effect rejecting not Samuel as a judge, but God, Himself, as their king. Israel up to this point a theocracy, a government with God as king, now changes to a monarchy as God gives the people a king in the man Saul.

While Saul starts out as a hesitant king, even hiding from the masses at the beginning, he becomes quite full of himself before long and falls out of favor with God by his blatant disobedience. Because of his rebellion, God chooses another to be king in Saul's place. The man God chooses is not a descendant of Saul, but a shepherd named David.

Before David becomes king, we hear of his exploits in killing the giant Goliath and of his deep friendship with Jonathan, King Saul's son, and of his first marriage to King Saul's daughter, Michal. Pursued ferociously by King Saul because he is perceived as such a threat to his kingdom, David lives on the edge for several years before King Saul finally takes his own life in battle and David ascends to the throne.

Called a "man after God's own heart," David's life exemplifies what it means to seek and follow God, with the exception of the Bathsheba incident. Bathsheba was married to one of David's soldiers, Uriah. One day, when David's men are out fighting wars, David is home in his palace. From his high vantage point, he sees Bathsheba bathing. Immediately taken by her beauty, David sends for her. One thing quickly leads to another and before long, David is sitting in a soap opera of adultery and murder, having offed Uriah upon receiving the news of Bathsheba's pregnancy.

The prophet Nathan calls David on his sin and David repents immediately. The damage having been done, David takes Bathsheba as another wife. After losing the baby conceived in adultery, Bathsheba eventually bears David his son, Solomon. Solomon succeeds his father David as king, but not before some of David's other sons, most notably Absalom, make a run at the throne.

It is Solomon who finally builds a permanent temple for the Lord. David had not been allowed to do this because, although he had followed God with all of his heart, he had been a man of bloodshed, a man of war. Solomon is best remembered for his wealth and his wisdom in ruling, but ironically, it is his lack of wisdom in the area of women that becomes his undoing.

Having wives and concubines that numbered in the hundreds, Solomon accommodated his foreign wives in the area of idol worship. Bad idea. Solomon is succeeded by his son, Rehoboam, who is not a good man. In fact, he is so bad that God tears a large portion of the kingdom out of his hand, leaving him only a small part because of His promise to David.

This is where it gets a little complicated, but once you grasp this, so much of the Old Testament will begin to hold together for you. Under Saul, David, and Solomon, Israel was one country with one king, the united monarchy with all 12 tribes of Israel under the king's control. When God pulls part of the kingdom away from Rehoboam, we move into the time of the divided monarchy. Rehoboam is still the king of what becomes known as the Southern Kingdom or Judah (comprised of the two tribes of Judah and Benjamin), while the Northern Kingdom or Israel (comprised of the other 10 tribes) is given to a man named Jeroboam. The capital of the Southern Kingdom is Jerusalem, the capital of the Northern Kingdom is Samaria. Details? Yes. Important? Extremely.

Until you grasp this flow of history around the division of the kingdom, much of the Old Testament history and prophecy will stay extremely muddy. With a reasonable understanding of this, however, you can jump in and read anywhere in the Old Testament with at least a degree of ease.

So, because of the importance of this, let's quickly review:

Northern Kingdom

Israel 10 Tribes

Non-Davidic

Capital: Samaria

Southern Kingdom

Judah 2 Tribes

Davidic Line

Capital: Jerusalem

Once the kingdom divides, a series of kings follow. The kings of Israel are bad. They are always bad. Not one of them is even remotely good. Israel, all bad, all the time.

The kings of Judah, on the other hand, are a mixed bag. Some are horrible, others okay, and at least one you could name a child after. More are bad than good, and most of the good ones still have reasonable shortcomings, but as a group they prove to be better than Israel, which is why the ax falls on them later than it does on their brothers to the North.

Elijah and Elisha prophesy during the time of the Divided Kingdom. The other prophets are sprinkled throughout the times of the monarchy, the captivity, and the post-exile period.

If you hate historical dates, you may be inclined to skip over the next section, but I implore you, please don't. Unlike most history that is fraught with countless crucial dates, there are only two dates that you need to remember in studying the Old Testament. The first is 722 BC, the second, 586 BC.

In 722 BC, the nation of Assyria conquered and deported the Northern Kingdom of Israel as was prophesied. After deporting Israel and dispersing them, Assyria resettled other people groups in the land of Israel. These people then intermarried with the remaining Israelites creating a half-breed people group referred to as Samaritans. This becomes significant in the New Testament as we see the intense hatred that the "purebred" Jews had for their half-breed brothers. Due to the deportation and intermixing of the Northern Kingdom, these tribes are often referred to as the 10 lost tribes of Israel.

Seeing their brothers carried away by Assyria does not have the impact on the Southern Kingdom that it should have. Although it takes a little longer and though there are pockets of revival along the way, notably that of King Josiah, eventually Judah goes the way of Israel. In 586 BC, Nebuchadnezzar conquers Judah and takes the people away into captivity in Babylon.

One of the people carried off to Babylon is Daniel. Probably the best known vegetable-eater of all time, Daniel, along with his three friends Shadrach, Meshach, and Abednego, were made servants in Babylon. Shadrach, Meshach, and Abednego were thrown into a fiery furnace when they refused to bow down to a golden statue only to be saved by the power of God. Daniel, likewise, was thrown into a den of lions because he continued to pray to his God, even when prayer to anyone but the king had been outlawed. He, too, was saved by the power of God.

After 70 years of captivity in Babylon, the people of Judah are released to go back to Jerusalem.

Nehemiah is in charge of rebuilding the wrecked walls of the city.

Between the end of the Old Testament and the beginning of the New Testament is a period of 400 years often referred to as the silent years.

With the Christ-event, God again speaks to His people beginning with His Word to Zechariah foretelling of the coming of John the Baptist who would prepare the way of the Lord.